FOR THE LOVE OF PETS

FOR THE LOVE OF
PETS

Contemporary Architecture
and Design for Animals

CONTENTS

6	**A Heartfelt Connection**
10	**CIRCLE OF LOVE** 360 Villa
16	**ON THE CATWALK** Anti-earthquake Cat House
22	**MI CASA, SU CASA** NeconoMa
26	**A WALK OF FUN** Casa de Gatos
32	**BOX-IN AND CHILL OUT** pidan cat bed
36	**GET CLIMBING** Geometric Climber-6 Gratings (cat tree)
40	**CHERRY ON THE CAKE** Cupcake pet bed
44	**SWINGING GOOD TIME** Hammock pet bed
48	**EARTH TO POOCH, OVER** Heads or Tails
52	**WHAT A SQUARE** Cubic pet goods
56	**FIT FOR ROYALTY** Cat's Moving Castle
60	**HOME-IN-ONE** D&C House
64	**NOOK FOR POOCH** Withrow Laneway House
70	**PUSS IN BOOKS** House for Booklovers and Cats
76	**A CUT ABOVE** Niku Rug (Architecture for Dogs)
80	**ALL ACCESS PASS** Sacha Apartment
84	**AWAKEN THE WILD** Juggernaut
88	**CHAMBER OF SECRET FUN** Neko Modern Cat Tree
92	**CORRUGATED PARADISE** Room Collection
98	**FULL HOUSE** Pets Playground
104	**HAVING A BALL** The Cube, The Ball
110	**HOW ABOUT A LIFT?** The Bed
114	**KITTY FROM THE BLOCK** Kitty Kasas Collection
118	**SKIP TO MY LU(LU), MY DARLING** Lulu bed
122	**UNDERCOVER COMFORT** Kikko table
126	**SNORING IN STYLE** Loue bed
130	**THE HIGH LIFE** Three Poles Cat Tower
134	**COUCH PETATO** Odense couch bed
136	**YOURS AND MINE** Oslo

138 **IN DA HOUSE** Small House Collection
142 **BEAM ME UP KITTY** MYZOO Spaceship cat bed
148 **CATNAP CANOPY** Canopy Bed
152 **CAT-RIUM OF BEAMS** Cat House
156 **FUREVER FUR-FREE** Bye Bye Fur
160 **SNAIL CAVE** Little Snail
164 **LEVEL-UP AND LET LOOSE** Cat Time Cat Tree
168 **KITTY WALK-UP** The Cat Flat
174 **OH, BUSY ME(OW)** MYZOO Busycat ottoman and shelf
180 **OUT ON THE TABLE** CATable 2.0
184 **SHELVE IT** Luna, Twinkle Star, and Moku
188 **IT'S FETCHING BRILLIANT** Fetch House (Architecture for Dogs)
192 **OFF WITH HIS CAGE** PAWD (Happy pet nesting space)
196 **PEEKABOO, I SEE YOU** Holey Moley
200 **REFLECTIONS OF LOVE** Yololand
204 **IN THE CENTER OF IT ALL** Sheridan Residence
208 **UNDER THE BRIDGE** sHome
212 **HAVEN OF HARMONY** Cats at Prince Charles
218 **ELECTRIC WITHOUT WIRES** Norrom Aquarium

222 **Project Credits**

A Heartfelt Connection

What would a household be without a pet? Most of us animal lovers and pet pawrents would rather not think about such an idea—the absence of little paws roaming the hallway with the accompanying clicketty-clicketting of pet nails, the chirp of a greeting on your return from work, or the exuberant tail-wagging excitement that only a dog can convey when their human is back with them—because life would be empty and glum without such things!

Around the world, and in varied residential spaces, a variety of non-human critters proudly hold the title "loved pet," from furry and feathered, to clawed and crawly, to finned and scaly; appearance means little and matters not, as long as the heart connection is strong.

And it is no news, given the results of many studies conducted, that a pet and its unconditional love and acceptance has the power to soften hearts, reduce stress, and relax a furrowed brow. Oh, and let's not forget a cat's purring. That's a whole other level of "therapy." If you make room in your heart for a pet, it's going to be there FURrrrever, because this is no two-day commitment; it's for the rest of pooch's and kitty's life.

For the love of pets, we definitely take pleasure in lavishing attention on our furmily members, spending huge and ever-increasing amounts of time and finances on their care, comfort, health, and happiness; not to mention the many toys, beds, and engagement tools. It also helps that there is a vast array of sophisticated pet products available in the marketplace today that reflects immense thought and care that has gone into their design. The projects in this book reveal the talents of designers from across the globe, including South Korea, Spain, France, Japan, The Netherlands, Sweden, and more, who deliver creations that are both stylish and just as equally functional and comfortable.

Interior and furniture designer, and founder of concept development company Designfolder, Eleonor Moschewitz, comments on the growing trend for affordable and stylish designs in pet furniture: "People are getting more aware of their homes; in Scandinavia, every home in urban areas looks like something out of a magazine. Interior design is growing and ordinary people are starting to buy into it. There's a lot of affordable designs on the market ... I think that has, and will, influence the pet product design industry."

"Design should be as simple as possible. But the hard part is to make it unique while keeping it simple. How can you make a product unique without adding something?" opines Onurhan Demir, industrial designer and creator of the Weelywally brand of pet furniture, revealing the presence of creativity and design exhibited in a vast amount of pet furniture today, resulting in desirable clean lines and styles that do not clash with the modern decor.

"The designed cat goods are usually not interesting for the cat ... so first I had to understand what a cat is ... Second, I had a brief to design a piece that could fit into a designer home and did absolutely not look like something that has been seen before," Moschewitz explains further.

The influence of the internet, the availability of more advanced, sophisticated materials, and the dedication of the design to the pet who would be using the furniture has certainly trained a more tasteful eye and discerning selection process among pet guardians when purchasing products for their pets; more of us care about the appearance of our homes and strive to find pieces that are unique and add personality and style, as well as speak volumes about our furry apple of our eye.

More experienced designers are turning to designing pet furniture and the results include some stylish projects in the book's line-up, such as The Cat Flat, Three Poles Cat Tower, and Neko Modern Cat Tree, which can be moved from room to room, as required, or, like the Geometric Climber-6 Gratings (cat tree), even serve a dual purpose as a cat play area and a bookcase. Whatever your taste, budget, or color scheme, there are varied selections of products to bring pleasure to your pet (MYZOO Busycat shelves) and inject vibrant color (Kitty Kasas Collection), or understated elegance to your home. A stylish occasional table (Kikko table) that includes a bed for kitty also functions as a useful piece of furniture, allowing both human and puss to spend more time together. Many of the designs feature a playful sense of humor too, such as the Niku Rug fashioned to resemble a steak, or the quirky Fetch House, adorned with tennis balls, perfect for a ball-obsessed puppy!

Fun and frolicking aside, there is no point to a pretty-looking pet palace if it is uncomfortable for your pet to be in it. And it is reassuring to know that these days, a lot of thought is also given to the emotion, comfort, and security of the pet when designing items specific to them. Some designers even seek out trained pet psychologists who offer insights into a pet's natural characteristics and behavior patterns, so that the pet furniture design can support these traits for maximum benefit to the pet. Knowing that a product has been designed by people who are pet/animal people themselves and has been tested by actual pets themselves is great news to a pet guardian because the value the item imparts is heightened.

"We conducted solid, very important research. We spoke with the best cat psychologist in Sweden, Susanne Hellman Holmström. In collaboration with her, we decided which features had to be taken into account so that the cabinet was created with the cats' well-being in mind all the time," reveals Viktoria Löwkrantz of PR and advertising company PostSthlm on The Cat Flat.

"We want the cabinet to add value to both the cat and the human. While it is attractive to look at, it at the same time fulfills cats' needs, such as hiding, scratching, spying, playing, and sleeping, without compromising design," she elaborates.

It is hardly surprising to find that a number of products, including Room Collection by A Cat Thing, or Juggernaut by Catastrophic Creations, are designed by animal lovers, who put their hours of observation to a constructive purpose, creating an environment that is both safe for the pet and inspires play, resulting in a contented and fulfilled animal.

"The design [of pet furniture] currently and down the road will be more from the pet's perspective, for their health and happiness; people will start paying more attention to them and what they need. People less and less are seeing their cats and dogs as 'pets,' but more like a friend and family member; this is crucially important because it would mean that people truly care for them," share husband-and-wife pet furniture designers A Cat Thing.

"Our cat, Lily, was very traumatized when we adopted her and her brother; they had to live with many other cats in the rescue center and then travel far away to our home when she was adopted. She refused to eat and drink for three days. When we were lost in panic, our friend who has two cats advised us to find her a cardboard box. We did it and she hid inside right away. Around an hour later, she emerged fresh! And started eating! That's the moment we started collecting cardboard boxes. We didn't think about making any product, we just wanted her to feel safe and happy."

"We started playing with boxes and made little buildings. We are both architects and so we have the passion for turning everything into architecture; gradually, we developed a module concept to make the whole structure neat and easy to assemble … It has to be easy and fun, and safe … another challenge is to make it look nice. As architects, we like to keep things stylish and minimal to make it a delightful object within every space … it's a constant test-and-error and an extremely time-consuming process; we made models for Chacha and Lily to try and they will show us what they like and don't like … They are the bosses!" says A Cat Thing.

For many designers, it was at such similar moments when the inspiration struck to design pieces after their own heart and own experiences as pet guardians. Reveals Demir, "I was locked at home for two months [due to the pandemic]. I aimed to create a unique collection that nobody would expect from something like pet furniture. I sold my car to finance this project."

Sustainability and safety also seem to be the paths many designers are taking, and will take, heading into the future, with material selection for pet products: "Natural woods and 100 percent cotton fabrics can keep our friends away from chemicals … There are also no sharp edges and corners in the designs to protect their eyes and faces," Demir continues.

"Sustainability thinking is a must! It has to be smart and safe too," says A Cat Thing.

It is clear that having love for the subject and a passion for what one does makes all the difference in striving for ultimate solutions in pet furniture that blend design and function. And this passion is demonstrated in the many dynamic projects that you will journey with in the pages ahead, browsing through stylish accents, creative concepts, and practical considerations that define current-day's pet furniture. But it doesn't stop there.

In these modern times, pet-tifying the home extends beyond simple pet products to include home architecture and design as well, and many creative solutions are employed to tailor the home for a pet's comfort, enjoyment, and engagement: such as a carpet wall to scurry up (Casa de Gatos), or an overhead bridge for active cats to keep occupied with (sHome), a raised perch so lovable canines can be eye-level with their humans (360 Villa), or portholes for shy felines to retreat into (House for Booklovers and Cats).

It is clear that there is no shortage of ingenious options. In some of the homes featured, cats are living it up and enjoying the many special home solutions that have been tailored just for them. Ranging from joinery work to create climbing areas, to catwalk rafter beams, to cat-path ledges, to carpet-covered walls for climbing, to sisal-covered columns as scratching posts, the creative explorations embarked on to design or renovate a home specifically for cats are wide and varied. Dogs get their day too, with a selection of works that honor the household's canine, with specially designed and built dog houses that form part of the architecture and decor, like in projects Sheridan Residence, Yololand, and Withrow Laneway House. And just like in pet furniture, these architecture and design modifications in both cat and canine households dig deep to consider a range of conditions to not only design dedicated spaces that match pooch's and kitty's personality and level of comfort, but also introduce playfulness into the aesthetics of the home.

Architect firm Studio North elaborates: "When considering our little fluffs during the design process, we always look for opportunities in the nooks and crannies. Normally, when designing a home, we only think about the scale of the human, so it takes a bit of a shift in thinking. We like to think of our pet as a client and understand what's important to them. I'm sure that everyone that is reading this book would agree that our pets are beloved family members and they should have a space to call their own. Just like humans, dogs and cats have personalities of their own. Some are claustrophobic and don't like to feel enclosed, while others like to climb and have a high perch; others insist on sleeping at the foot of the bed. All of these are important things to consider when designing for our furry friends. We know that a dog wants to be somewhere that they can watch everything that's going on in the house since they consider themselves as the 'protector of the pack.' They also want to have a space that is cozy, secure, and close to their family. Quite often, depending on the size of our pet we find places in millwork, under desks, carving out a stud space, built into a bed frame, etc."

Commenting on the project Withrow Laneway House, they had this to say, "We knew that the dog house was going to be for a small Pomeranian named Spencer, so the scale of the nook was already determined. Spencer likes a cozy nook to sleep in and is a dedicated guard dog. We wanted to find a very central location in the house and so incorporated it into the millwork feature wall. The neat aspect of the dog house is that it's built into the cabinet on the other side of the wall in the bedroom, so when the cabinet door is open, it also serves as a passage into the bedroom. This way Spencer can be close to his family both during sleep at night and during the activities of the day … It is always a fun design challenge, since pets come in all shapes and sizes, and personalities. They make for an exciting client to design for! It allows us to be really playful with making the most out of space."

When it comes to our pets, "creature comforts" is something of an understatement and, truthfully, just the start of it. There is almost no task or acquisition that is "over the top" when ensuring a nurturing and fulfilling environment for our special nuzzle buds. With many home floor plans shrinking in size, imaginative pet furniture designs present function, with a welcome heaping of aesthetic and style, as Löwkrantz highlights.

"Every cat has thirteen 'necessity' needs that need to be fulfilled in order for a cat to feel good and be satisfied in their home … cats are very popular pets and people tend to forget that they have a lot of wild instincts carried through in their DNA. One thing that every cat owner should take into consideration is to offer the cat possibilities to spy, hunt, and give them a place where they can hide. It can be hard for an indoor cat to do these kinds of things when living in a small space area."

"With urbanization, higher housing prices, and overcrowding, we see that many indoor cats do not have the opportunity to have their natural needs fulfilled and thus start to act different and can become depressed … This book could help people get inspired on how to create their own furniture plan and it is wonderful to be able to combine benefit with pleasure. At the same time, as you make room in your home for the right priorities, you also get an interior design dream!"

The ability to keep your cherished fur family happy and contented is indeed a gift. And a beautiful home, on top of melting puppy-dog eyes or a curled-up cat (or, if you prefer, cats) purring on your lap, is a definite bonus to a pet guardian's days. Pets are increasingly taking prominence in many households and the impact of their unconditional love and calming presence—be they rescued or adopted—is a well-known and appreciated privilege. It's hard to compare anything to the fulfillment of a furry tail slumped across your outstretched legs, connected to the contented fur-baby sprawled on the couch next to you.

The projects featured in this book acknowledge the importance of our furry, feathered, scaly, and finned family, and also admits, and without shame too, that nothing is too radical or out of this world when it comes to our darling pets.
Because with pets, it is truly the heart that speaks.

CIRCLE OF LOVE

Name: 360 Villa
Design: 123DV
Photography: Hannah Anthonysz

When you love your pets, "lavish attention" is an understatement. And what better way than a 360-degree visual of them—even when they are outdoors—no matter what pet and person are up to.

This circular home in The Netherlands, tailored to connect two Alaskan malamutes and their people, is built with glass walls so the residents can give their beloved dogs all the attention and contact they ask for, both inside and outside the home. The ceiling, which also forms the roof of the home, cleverly reaches out beyond the home's exterior to create an eave-like extension that skirts the perimeter of the house to provide shelter for the dogs when they are lounging outdoors.

Outside the bedroom and kitchen, the garden rises to a hillock that crests at mid-height of the façade to create an area where the dogs can be at eye level with their humans, so that they can look each other in the eye, to keep the connection strong. The mound also provides privacy at the home's street side.

With love and adoration like this, there is no such thing as too much. Mirrors on either end of the terrace widen the angles of visual contact, so pets and people are always in each other's company even if not beside each other.

Though modest in size, the novel design of this home in the forest creates an openness and freedom that the home owners happily share with their two precious dogs.

ON THE CATWALK

Name: Anti-earthquake Cat House
Design: Hitotomori Architects
Photography: Hiroki Kawata

Every cloud has a silver lining. Renovating this home in Japan to include a series of anti-earthquake support braces was a challenge when it came to creating usable spaces for the family but it produced a fun, rich environment for the family's cats.

The house, home to a mother and daughter, and their two cats, was renovated to extend its lifespan and stability for another forty years. The cracks in the wall were repaired, the roof was lightened and the structure was made earthquake-proof, all without altering the appearance of the home, or the way in which the family used the home, so as to maintain the memory of the family's late patriarch.

While the wooden supports used for structural reinforcement to improve the home's seismic performance resulted in an aesthetic and spatial challenge, the resident cats love them.

The high beams are now fancy catwalks, which the cats can't get enough of, criss-crossing from one end to another, traipsing about, and exploring the space. As cats always do, they enjoy being above everybody else, perched high on the beams with their noses in the air—quite literally, in this case.

Transparent partitions are placed amid the beams above doorways and door frames to mimic a division of space in the cats' quarters. Little cat-sized doorways are cut out into these partitions so the cats can move freely between rooms and follow their people around the house, but still enjoy their own space.

MI CASA, SU CASA

Name: NeconoMa

Design: Alegre Design (for Katzden Architec)

Photography: Pablo Bosch

There is no cat that doesn't love a high perch from which it can have its eyes on the world *and* its person. Oh, and of course, where it can snooze.

The NeconoMa wall-mounted modular series of perches and cradles creates entertainment for feline furmily members just as it allows them to indulge in their natural characteristics of jumping, climbing, and, most importantly, perching high and overlooking the world.

Shaped like houses, the cat perches promote psychological and physical well-being, with elements that cater to natural feline behavior. Cats are sure to enjoy the cozy fit of the frame and the overhead roof, nestling into their "house" quite contentedly. Portholes on the side wall and roof (depending on the design variety) also cater to their curious, playful nature because we all know: if there is an opening, the cat will stick its head in; if there is a tight space, it will squeeze into it; and if there is a roof or any protrusion resembling one, the cat will most definitely sit under it.

24

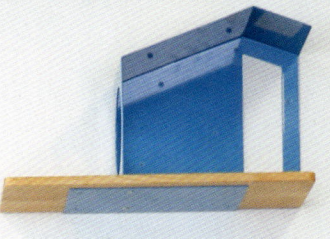

The series also includes cradles that provide snug snooze spots, which the cat will have no difficulty getting comfortable in. The modular system of the NeconoMa allows the freedom to create different varieties of a fun and engaging system that motivates play, facilitates exercise, and, at the same time, provides rest areas, so that when the cat gets tired of you and she's "over it," she can retreat to her private cubbyhole perch for some much-needed, not to mention deserved, cat me-time, for it can be oh-so-exhausting being cat-fabulous.

A WALK OF FUN

Name: Casa de Gatos
Design: WOWOWA Architecture
Photography: Martina Gemmola

This contemporary Mexican-themed home in Melbourne, Australia named "house of cats" in Spanish (Casa de Gatos) shelters two adults, two dogs, and two—you guessed it—cats. The result of a second renovation on a Victorian worker's cottage, the home optimizes design, a play of light, and multiuse furniture to tailor a comfortable space fit for all six inhabitants.

The frisky felines are kept happily occupied with an extruded dado rail that forms a ledge for them to walk along. This hanging rail runs along the corridor to the main bedroom and bathroom, and around the bathroom pod. Add to that a Tretford carpet wall and it's party time for the active cats who enjoy scaling the wall in their rambunctious play.

Made from 150-year-old reclaimed timber from old CSR sugar mills, the dado rail also features semi-circular cutouts for the cats to dart from the carpet-wall to their cool cat walkway.

The two pooches get in on the fun too, relaxing in the breezy open spaces created by smart design and even smarter furniture, such as an integrated joinery system that contains home essentials and appliances, among other things, within a neat assembly. This helps to save floor space, especially within a modest footprint, leaving more for the household's animals to lounge in.

Abundant light flooding in from the windows fills the areas in the home with sunshine, keeping good vibes all around for both people and paws. Enjoying the light atmosphere, the dogs ready themselves for the evening's entertainment: two zany cats scurrying up the walls.

BOX-IN AND CHILL OUT

Name: pidan cat bed
Design: pidan
Photography: pidan

Created by pet product designer pidan, this cat bed (also suitable for a small dog) provides a great experience for companion animals, while checking off functionality and aesthetics.

Anyone who shares their days with a cat will tell you: cats love their naps. And this bed ensures they'll have very pleasant kitty dreams, snuggled in its comfortable surrounds. Thermal bending technology creates a curved box-shaped frame without hard, pointy corners that might challenge the art of curling up.

Made with a single piece of laminate without any joining points, the contours of the bed provide a sense of wrapping that supports cats' curled-up sleeping positions—a good substitute for those rainy nights when your lap is busy with popcorn and the remote. It's most suited to the size of cat, but a small dog would also enjoy this comfortable bed in a minimalist design.

The smooth finish of the wood base is easy to clean and maintain, and cushions in a layered arrangement provide support for the pet's head and body, or can be removed to fill the bed with a rug or throw that your pet loves. The cushion cover can also be removed and laundered, making sure kitty's bed is always spick and span; the non-slip silicone base of the cushions makes sure they stay in place as your cat stretches, rolls over, and repeats. It's certainly a hard life as a cat.

GET CLIMBING

Name: Geometric Climber-6 Gratings (cat tree)
Design: pidan
Photography: pidan

On first look, this confusing maze of squares looks like an impressive, avant-garde bookshelf. Put a cat on it and one soon realizes that it is, in fact, a really fun and unusual cat tree that is, yes, also a bookshelf—if you want it to be.

Different-sized square wood frames fit together through a mortise-and-tenon assembly system to customize a variety of patterns to the fancy of you and your cat (more his than yours). Being modular, the system can also be split and spread across different areas in the home to create more play areas for the cat, which puss will love.

Each square frame features circular openings and when assembled together as a unit, the openings become portals that he can crawl and climb through in his explorations to access the different areas and levels of the geometric climber. The design creates multiple planes interspersed with semi-enclosed nooks and perches for puss to go wild.

While the cat is having its fun, you can have yours too, arranging displays of things you love. With plenty of stacking space, this geometric climber can also be a bookshelf and plant stand; and we're sure puss won't mind you borrowing a little space. Plus, the filled-up spaces encourage him to consider alternative routes on his jaunts, exercising his mind as well as his limbs. However, be sure not to block off pathways, such that puss has to do a *Mission Impossible*, which could risk his safety—we're not all Tom Cruise. A few pots of microgreens or cat grass along the way make a healthy snack for your curious feline as he takes to his climb.

CHERRY ON THE CAKE

Name: Cupcake pet bed
Design: pidan
Photography: pidan

If you've always thought of your fluffy little miss as the cherry on your cake, now she can be—a cute, cuddly, cat-shaped cherry.

Fulfilling all the requisites of comfort, this playful Cupcake pet bed invokes memories of delectable confections and presents an annoyingly adorable picture when a cuddly pet is snuggled on top—it's really more of an indulgence designed for you than for your pet. And if you've always wanted a pet bed to complement your Strawberry Shortcake decor, you've got yourself one.

The deep base of the bed (cupcake liner) fashions a high brim around your pet, which creates a feeling of "nestling in" each time your kitty or little pooch settles into the bed. This provides your pet with security and comfort; never a bad thing.

If your little cuddle-bug is more the vivacious sort who likes to see and be seen and not the tuck-away-and-disappear type, you can easily raise the cupcake base with double cushions so little miss can still have her eye on things while she gets some shut-eye.

The 100 percent premium polyester fiber cushion has a removable cover that can be laundered, so it's no sweat keeping the bed clean for your fussy miss. You could even get new cushion covers stitched to design a variety of colorful cake bases to place a cute kitty- or pooch-shaped cherry on top.

SWINGING GOOD TIME

Name: Hammock pet bed
Design: pidan
Photography: pidan

Ever heard the saying, "The cat has the best seat in the house"? Well, it's true. And this Hammock pet bed creates reasons to be envious, if we don't say so ourselves.

Designed to occupy minimum space yet provide a comfortable siesta spot for your pampered little miss or mister, the Hammock pet bed is almost invisible in your interior with its sleek form and proportions. Three poles form a tripod-like stand between which is a comfortable, durable piece of cloth that extends as the cot.

A copper-alloy screw system ensures the hammock is stable, even if kitty moves about in her sweet slumber, dreaming of fish treats and chasing butterflies. The hammock is also perfect for days when she just wants to stretch out, show you her belly and peer at you cutely, secretly Jedi mind-controlling you to walk over and give her a belly rub.

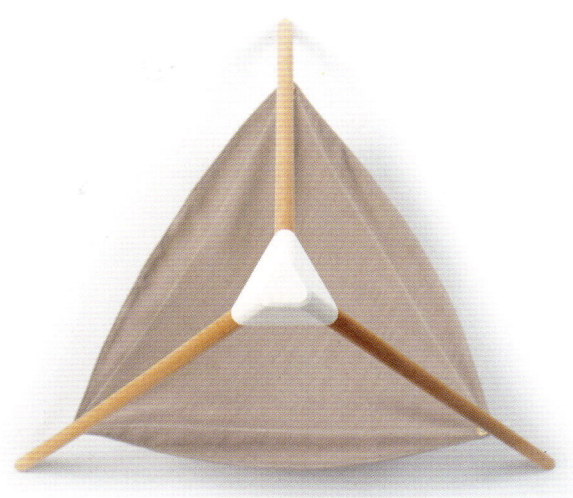

Made of beech, each wooden pole is heat-treated and surface-treated with eco-friendly wax, without formaldehyde, so you know your kitty is safe even if she gnaws at the poles in her frisky play. The curved, pocket-center of the cot allows room to roll and also creates a comfortable "suspended" feeling that cats love in a hammock. Incidentally, one of ours loves crawling into the grocery bag hanging on a hook by the window, but the hammock is certainly more fashionable and safer, perfect for your little miss.

EARTH TO POOCH, OVER

Name: Heads or Tails
Design: nendo
Photography: Akihiro Yoshida

Your adventurous pooch will love this dog hut that looks right out of a science fiction movie. Locking like an outer-space base set up by space explorers, this hut will make your dog feel like a space trooper.

Part of an innovative collection by nendo, which plays on forms and shapes, the hut can be converted into a cushy dog bed with a simple flatten-and-tuck—very space-age indeed, bringing to mind transforming robots, spaceships, and even people. The collection also includes a dog dish, which is a shallow food bowl one way up and a deep water bowl the opposite way up, as well as a rubber bone toy, which is also a ball.

The magic is in the construction of triangle panels connected in a polygon mesh that allow for each item to be easily reshaped into a different item, except for the dog dish of course, which needs only a simple flip to serve its dual purpose.

The collection comes in both black and white to harmonize with different home interiors and different coat colors (always a must). The hut in synthetic leather is plush both as a hut to tuck away into and a bed to sprawl on top of, making for a comfortable, restful sleep for pooch in either form, as he ventures deep into space in his intergalactic dreams.

WHAT A SQUARE

Name: Cubic pet goods
Design: nendo
Photography: Akihiro Yoshida

We love pet beds that can be configured into multiple designs and we think you would too.

The Cubic dog bed is something of a chameleon, able to change its look to suit the occasion, the mood of pooch, and the size of your household—just in case your household were to grow by another set of paws.

The dog bed is part of the Cubic pet goods collection created to step away from the typical circular designs that mark most dog products and accessories, to present the market with something stylish and different, and which can match more seamlessly with interior spaces in a linear design.

Minimalist, stylish, and different from the usual, the 3D, geometric form of the Cubic dog bed catches the eye and emphasizes its compatibility with a variety of interiors. Not to mention, it shakes things up in the decor some. Plus, both you and pooch can have fun with it, because it can be a cube dog house for those rainy days with no walks, or squashed down and configured into a base for a comfy bed for pooch's summer siesta.

And if you decide to get pooch a playmate, don't sweat it. Unfasten the zipper around the center of the dog house and voilà–it becomes two dog beds! This fun, creative design also lets you combine different color halves to create one-of-a-kind looks to match your decor and your pooches' personalities—mauve for Daddy's girl and beige for the indifferent snorer.

FIT FOR ROYALTY

Name: Cat's Moving Castle

Design: Hangzhou Furrytail Technology Co., Ltd.

Photography: Hangzhou Furrytail Technology Co., Ltd.

If you have ever felt bad about leaving the cat at home while you head out for some downtime, banish the thought because now kitty can come too, and still look as sleek and collected as she does lounging at home in bed.

The Cat's Moving Castle is a pet bed and a carrier in one. Instead of having to "go to war" just to get the cat into its carrier, here you flip the capsule's cover closed while the cat is in bed and you're all set to step outside to take in the sights and sounds with your cuddle-bug. When you're at home and the Moving Castle is in bed mode, a secure tab anchors the open cover and hinge caps ensure there is no discomfort to a sprawling cat.

A carrier sometimes presents itself as a foreign, ominous item as it's often stored away until needed. Since the Cat Castle is also a bed, kitty travels with familiar scents, which goes a long way in keeping her calm. The spherical shape of the cabin is also conducive for the cat to relax comfortably in and she is not confined to resting on her haunches.

We all know how cats love to watch—birds, bugs, people, just about everything, really—and how every small movement is a visual stimulation, especially with their super sight. The wide transparent cover makes a trip to the park with you an absolute joy as she takes in every shiver of leaf, sway of branch, even flutter of wing, all without the slightest ruffling of fur.

HOME-IN-ONE

Name: D&C House
Design: Kononenko ID
Photography: Andrii Podorozhny

Furniture that is for both paws and people? Oh, yes please! When at home, there is almost nothing better than having your loved furry friend around you all the time (except maybe having two furry friends!).

Pet beds tucked away in a dark corner of the home are becoming a thing of the past with units such as the D&C House, which integrates your pet's personal space into yours, so that you can be around each other as much as possible. We know kitty would love that for sure, for what superior creature wouldn't want its servants to be in waiting all the time?

The D&C House is a multifunctional solution in furniture—as a pet bed, table, and storage unit for pet supplies in one. It provides pooch and kitty with their own space while still being at the heart of the action. Built with high-quality material and hypoallergenic fabric for the upholstery, this pet house is made to last and will make memories for you and your loved pet companion for years to come.

An eye-catching, functional design paired with a variety of contemporary finishes allows this unit to blend with both modern and eclectic interiors. It makes a great console, or a side table for your mug in your cozy reading corner, *and* it has a cuddly friend tucked away within. What more could you need?

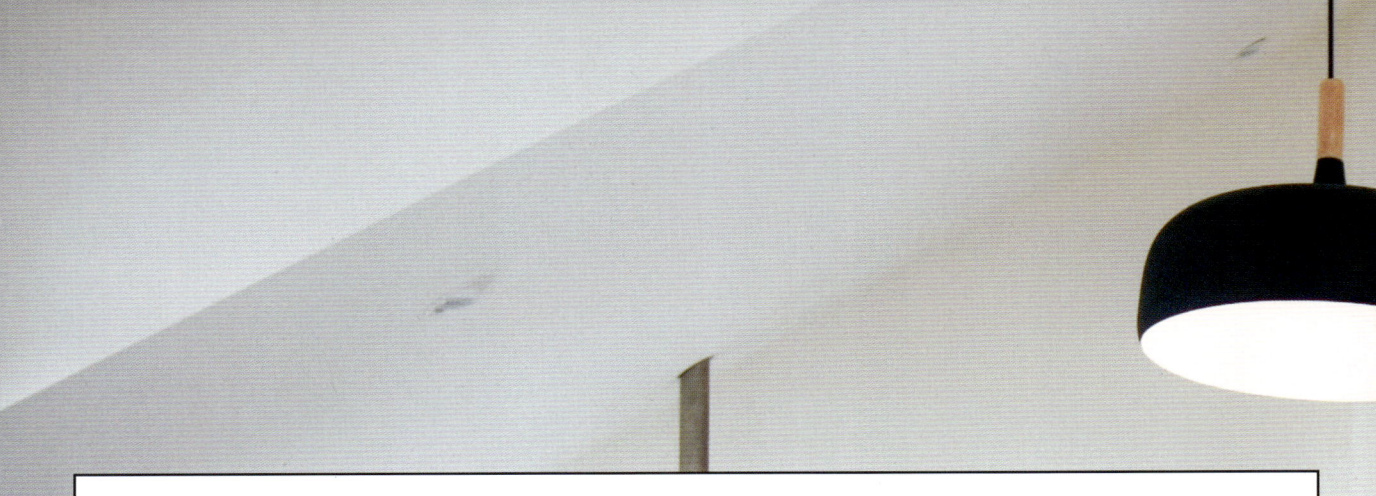

NOOK FOR POOCH

Name: Withrow Laneway House
Design: Studio North
Photography: Studio North

Tailoring one's home architecture for your feline family often seems easier than doing the same for your canine family; there seem more elements to create for cats, given that they present as more multifaceted. No doubt, dogs are at heart and soul simple beings; they are happy just to be near you. It does not mean, however, that you can't get just as creative in designing your home around them.

This two-story laneway house in Calgary, Canada puts together a selection of fun designs to build a happy and thoughtful abode for a beloved pooch and its humans. Part of a two-phase development plan for a riverfront property, this home is a new construction in the backyard of an existing home that has roads along both its front and rear, hence its description "laneway house." Though constructed on a budget and with a modest floor area, the home design does not leave out the comfort of the dog.

Among playful inclusions like a reading loft accessed by a ladder and a salvaged fireman's pole that can be used to zip down to the first floor, the design incorporates a cozy dog nook in the open-plan sitting area, so Spencer the dog can be near his favorite people. The dog nook, accessed by a circular opening in the wall, is built into the wall, creating a personal space where Spencer can feel secure and retreat into for a time-out.

It also extends as a shortcut—or as we prefer to think of it, an exciting secret passageway—through the cabinet on the other side of the wall to access the bedroom—his very own secret tunnel. The design considers a dog's natural ancestral instinct of burrowing into a nest when it wants to rest, making this dog nook an appealing and inviting spot that is just for pooch, right next to the family as his humans catch up on some relaxing television time.

PUSS IN BOOKS

Name: House for Booklovers and Cats
Design: Barker Associates Architecture Office
Photography: Francis Dzikowski

If there be books, there be shelves, and you know what that means: play space for adventurous felines. Extending that concept, this home incorporates a few other complementing elements to create fulfillment and contentment in the days of the household's adored kitties.

Combining color and light to create suitable spaces for its occupants, this row house in New York, United States also indulges two shy, inquisitive cats with high perches and quick "duck-outs" to escape unfamiliar guests. The cat walkway trails the top of a full-wall bookshelf in the main living space and is accessed by steps composed by protruding shelves.

This open walkway presents a high vantage point from which the kitties can watch from a distance first before deciding whether to partake, making impromptu gatherings and visits by guests less stressful than they could be. Should the activities not be to their taste, trapdoors on either end of the walkway that connect to the rooms upstairs allow them to stealthily slink off to more suited engagements without a hair out of place.

On days when the sun is out, the skylight and large floor-to-ceiling windows invite the sun's warmth and light into the living space toasting up the cats' favorite nooks in the house for a carefree bask, usually accompanied with a captivating series of languid, uninhibited poses that would put any supermodel to shame.

A CUT ABOVE

Name: Niku Rug (Architecture for Dogs)

Design: MAD Architects

Photography: Hiroshi Yoda

When we love our pets with genuine devotion, pampering them in sometimes unusual ways is, well, nothing unusual. In the name of pet love, many of us have indulged in our fair share of over-the-top acts that would have certainly raised more than a few eyebrows.

Arranging a "slab of meat" on the living room floor certainly qualifies as well, but as we say, "If pooch loves it, we love it!"

Designed as part of the Architecture for Dogs series, Niku Rug makes for a great play and rest zone for your fun-loving hound as you enjoy each other's company. Shaped like meat, it also reflects the idea in name, "*niku*" being the Japanese translation of the word "meat." Befitting the rug's quirky shape and design, the name is also humorously straight to the point; the gag really comes through when you behold your playful pooch innocently gnawing on the corners of the over-sized chop—it definitely hits high on the amusement scale.

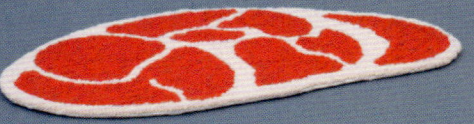

A three-color palette creates a remarkable likeness, even capturing the marbling in a cut of meat. The design is inspired by how we love to pamper our lolloping canines with a juicy steak treat and embodies the concept as a treat of comfort, with soft wool that your dog will contentedly delight in as he settles down next to you to get into his usual antics. Available in three sizes to suit all sizes of paws, the rugs can also be easily moved as your loyal tail-thumping fan follows you around the home to be near you and keep watch on his doggy *steak*out.

ALL ACCESS PASS

Name: Sacha Apartment
Design: SABO project
Photography: Alexandre Delaunay

While we love our cats, we also know they can be stubborn. Even when you say "no," they blatantly ignore you and find a way to disobey. The sneaky ones calculatedly bide their time and wait for when you are not looking to make their dash to liberation. The rebellious ones show you who's truly boss and go for it right under your nose, creating notoriously funny scenarios in the process.

In response, this duplex in Paris, France designs interior elements to create boundaries where they are needed and allow freedom where it can be had. A spiral staircase connects the two levels, with the lower floor housing the bedrooms; this area is also out of bounds to the cat. To ensure that the tenacious feline gets the message, the staircase access on the second floor is hidden behind a curved door. Result: kitty is none the wiser and no funny business shall be had.

In contrast, the living space on the second floor is all for the cat. Kitty gets to go where kitty pleases, when kitty pleases, with special cat accesses—arched openings in partitions and doors that allow her to access areas in the home even when they are otherwise sealed off.

There is even a cozy nook within the kitchen cupboard for kitty to slink away into, because, as we know, cats are tolerant of us humans only for so long and they often mysteriously leave the scene to retreat to hiding spots unknown to us. Through another kitty access in the cupboard, the cat enters her private cave (location classified) for a blissful snooze undisturbed by her humans.

AWAKEN THE WILD

Name: Juggernaut
Design: Catastrophic Creations
Photography: Michael Wilson

Part of the fun of being a pet guardian is creating play options for our pets, which they will enjoy. With a feline furmily, that's usually building a cat wall. You get to tailor the wall to your cat's personality and customize the units to his fitness level and athletic ability. For example, lower shelves for a senior cat to protect his joints, or wider jumps for an active young 'un who loves leaping like he's got wings.

The Juggernaut cat wall complex contains everything a cat loves: hammocks, a cat bridge, floating scratch posts, climbing poles, jumping platforms, snoozing lounges, and planters (for cat-friendly plants), which can also work as treat/feeding stations to make puss feel like he is hunting for his food—an instinct that has by now definitely been revealed, courtesy of the bug parts that occasionally decorate your floors.

The system is designed by cat guardians themselves who spend a lot of time interacting with and observing their own cats, who obligingly test each prototype before it is included in the product list. It is an environment of enrichment that provides your feline with outlets to himself reacquaint with his natural behavior. The convenient modular design also allows you to expand Juggernaut with any other cat wall component by Catastrophic Creations.

When a cat is stimulated with a variety of experiences that encourage its innate instincts, it's less likely to feel anxiety or aggression or display behavioral issues. The best part of a cat wall is the fulfillment and joy you get from watching your cat enjoy himself on it, making like he's a wild jaguar in the jungle—it's warm, fuzzy, and all love.

CHAMBER OF SECRET FUN

Name: Neko Modern Cat Tree
Design: Yoh Komiyama Design
Photography: Tomooki Kengaku

Cats have always had minds of their own: make them a bed in a warm, quiet corner, and they'll snooze on the hutch; lovingly buy them a mouse toy, and they'd rather kick around your socks. Some days you just can't win. But not with the Neko cat tree.

Not your usual carpeted tower, the Neko cat tree in hardwood is artistic, elegant, and a little cheeky. The doweled exterior acts like a screen that provides cover for your cat's naughty antics, but still makes your fluffy partner in crime visible to extend that soul connection. Puss will love the peekaboo effect too, as he slyly reaches his soft paws to get you through the bars as you walk by.

The tunnel-like chamber of the cylindrical design speaks to cats' love of playing in "secretive" concealed spaces, and your mischief-maker will enjoy entertaining himself climbing and jumping about within, feeling like he's hidden from the world and free to let his inner imp out. When your whiskered munchkin is all played out, there is ample room on the platforms to snooze and rest.

When the sun is out, the platforms become ideal basking spots—the dowel-screen allows just enough sun through so kitty is sprinkled with its warm glow, but still comfortable in filtered shade. The marble base—inspired by a cat spotted sprawled on the floor outside a house, using the very floor to cool himself—adds a refinement in its unusual incorporation and makes a great spot for your furry pal to sprawl and chill.

CORRUGATED PARADISE

Name: Room Collection
Design: A Cat Thing
Photography: Heycheese

Every cat is different with its own unique personality. Some like high platforms, some like dark corners, and then there are some that like the bathroom sink (we speak from experience on this one). But if there is one thing they *all* love, it's cardboard! If it's cardboard, they're there—sitting, rolling, lying down, and doing whatever else cats do with cardboard and looking cheek-pinchingly adorable doing it.

The humble cardboard might hardly be fancy, but as cat furniture, it's an absolute winner. Plus, it's also eco-friendly and sustainable, so it's double the happy knowing that you're helping the environment.

The Room Collection is a set of four cardboard modules that can be stacked any way you want, to create a cat bungalow for your playful fluffball to let loose and be a cat, jumping, crawling through openings, climbing, and scratching.

More modules can be added to expand kitty's play space, which is held securely in place with connections fashioned on the principles of origami. The modules are designed to manage high payloads, so even if your beloved tail-swisher is a chubby one, the little dear can still thrill in the joy of the Room Collection.

Assembly instructions are simple and easy to follow, so no screw will be left behind (this little mishap, too, from experience). Every part of the product and packaging is recyclable and non-toxic, so even if kitty were to get into any bits in her enthusiasm, there need be no interruption to her play and she can continue her scooting about without skipping a beat.

FULL HOUSE

Name: Pets Playground
Design: Sim-Plex Design Studio
Photography: Patrick Lam

You know a household is serious about its pet/s when the home interior is specially designed to serve the comfort, pleasure, and safety of their loved non-human family.

This home in Hong Kong, China accommodates a couple, a mother, a cat, and a parakeet, and cleverly crafts its interior to extend to each party their private space, as well as create communal spaces that pets and people can share.

Pets are most content when they are engaged and comfortably rested (not forgetting mealtimes with their favorite food and lots of love and cuddles). Step-shelves, cat cabins, nooks, and walkways in the cabinetry in the kitchen and the mother's room define interesting cat routes for the curious feline to explore and choose as worthy nap spots.

In the mother's room, where the cat usually sleeps, step-shelves in the overhead cabinet lead to a catwalk at the top of the unit to indulge a cat's natural instinct to seek out a high perch. On days when the cuddly darling is feeling less active, a cat house in the wardrobe opposite makes an ideal nook to curl up in, command time to stand still, and simply enjoy being a cat.

The parakeet's den is set in the living room before a large window facing west to catch the sun and natural light. And because we are all familiar with the antics of Sylvester and Tweety, fritted glass doors section off the living room when this feathered cutie is out and about for a flutter to stretch its wings. Other safety considerations in the home include ecological melamine-faced wooden furniture with lower formaldehyde to keep this paws-and-people family healthy and happy.

HAVING A BALL

Name: The Cube, The Ball
Design: Meyou Paris
Photography: Meyou Paris

Pet beds have come a long way since they were a simple nest of old rags in a warm corner, or a worn-out cushion under the table; now they are furniture that you include as part of your home design. The Meyou Paris range of cat beds prides itself on tailoring comfortable cat furniture that also feeds your appreciation of beautiful form.

Composed in natural materials—so natural, it's handwoven—the Meyou Paris range presents cozy cat beds that deliver elegance, while speaking to the innate nature of your little panther. Curved forms create ideal hiding spaces that appeal to the predatory instinct of your cat, allowing him to "stalk" the humans in his surroundings without being noticed. The cradling quality of the spherical shapes also make for most gratifying naps.

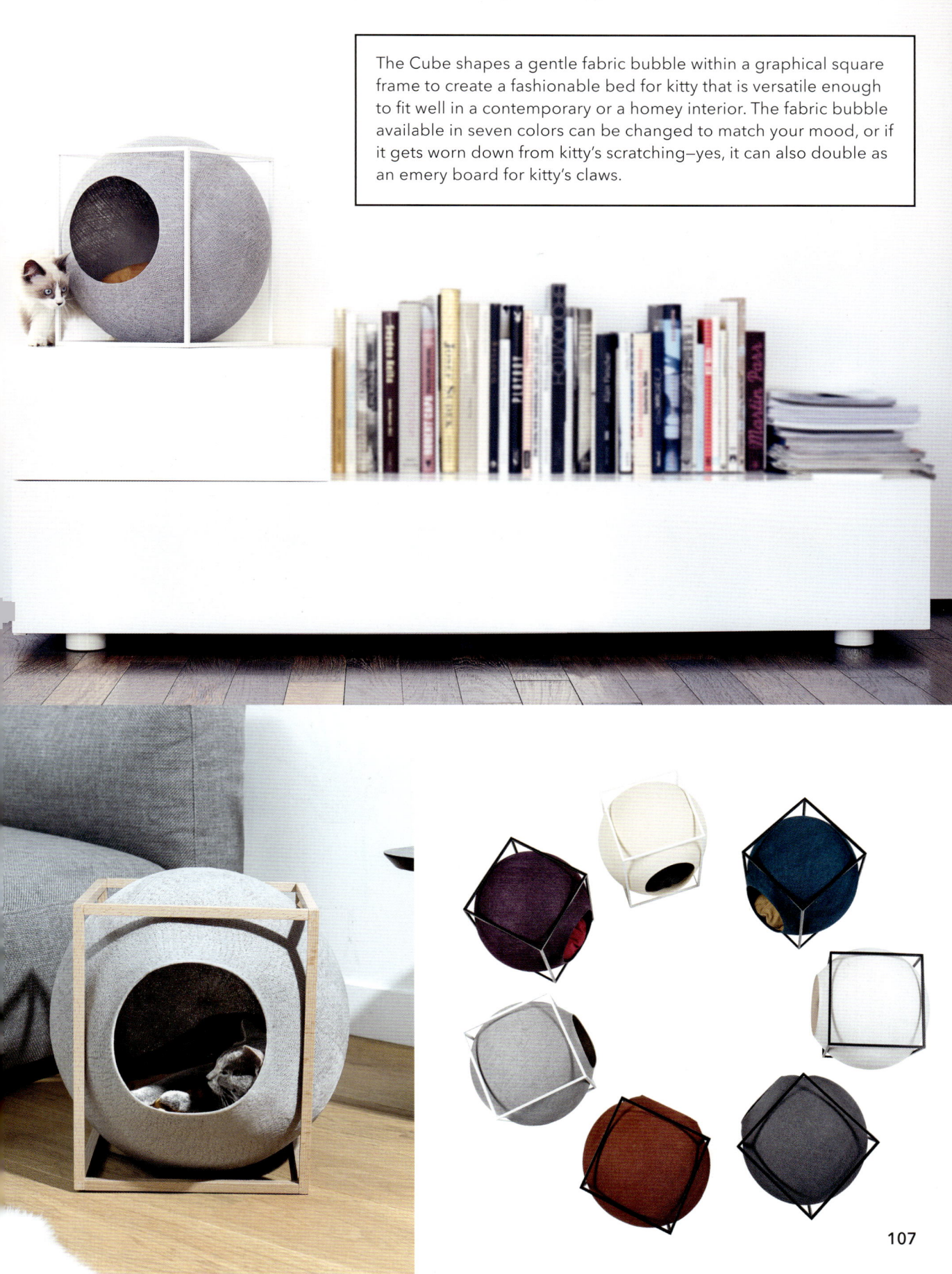

The Cube shapes a gentle fabric bubble within a graphical square frame to create a fashionable bed for kitty that is versatile enough to fit well in a contemporary or a homey interior. The fabric bubble available in seven colors can be changed to match your mood, or if it gets worn down from kitty's scratching—yes, it can also double as an emery board for kitty's claws.

The Ball, also available in seven colors, sits a handwoven cotton cocoon on a solid beech-and-metal stand to present an alternative design with the same stylish characterizations. Like The Cube, the handwoven cocoon can be removed and changed when the color scheme of your interior changes, so that while you are enjoying your new decor, your little predator can still enjoy the familiarity of a well-loved bed, even if the "jungle" outside is a little different.

HOW ABOUT A LIFT?

Name: The Bed
Design: Meyou Paris
Photography: Meyou Paris

Cats enjoy vantage points, and even more so if they have an element of seclusion. This often means navigating a swishing tail and a stubborn rear end to retrieve your loose change and keys from under that five kilograms of stealth perched on your dresser. Or opening the refrigerator for a midnight snack and getting a heart-stopping scare, courtesy of two luminous ghostly eyes peering at you from the top.

To save us from further terror, cat furniture designs today, thankfully, consider kitty's natural behavior and tailor elements to appeal. This elevated cat bed is one such answer.

With a raised perch and a canopy dome, this offering from Meyou Paris will be hard to pass up—for both your cat and you—as it coos feline luxury, pet comfort, and sophisticated style. Kitty needs no invitation here, enthusiastically taking to the high bunk with its canopy cover, where she can perch to get her eyeful and still feel like she's hidden and inconspicuous.

Reminiscent of a gramophone horn, the dome tapers toward the back and joins with the base to create a snug pocket, which your pampered feline will appreciate on rainy days, or even on hot days, when she can tuck herself away in the shade of the recess.

The dome is interchangeable and can be rotated between three color options to match an often-changing decor, or even other Meyou cat beds (page 104) to create different napping environments for your favorite ankle hunter.

KITTY FROM THE BLOCK

Name: Kitty Kasas Collection (by Kitty Kasas)

Design: Studio Mango

Photography: Kitty Kasas

If you've ever fantasized about a kitty pad within your own pad, here's proof someone else had that same fantasy.

Bringing a fresh approach to pet product design, the Kitty Kasas Collection allows you to create a kitty universe especially for your pampered princess, where she can lounge, get her steps in, play till she drops, and just be keepin' it fresh.

The collection of box-like playhouses includes bedrooms, recreation rooms in different designs (with hanging toys), and what we dub "nail rooms," with sisal-scratch poles for her claws. You can create different varieties of kitty pads simply by stacking together different designs of playhouses and accessories in the collection. If kitty is a nap queen, you can include more bedroom playhouses in your kitty pad; if she is a hyperactive grasshopper, you can accommodate her by creating more levels with more recreation rooms. The flat surfaces also ensure stability in the construction, so your excited kitty, enthusiastically conquering her "mountain" to get to the top, will be safe at all times.

116

The modular design is easy to add to if needed—to build your cuddly queen her very own theme park, or trim down her penthouse if space is an issue, saving you the dilemma of having to choose between your family heirloom piece of furniture, or kitty's first-floor bedroom extension. Stacking the playhouses upward also lets you limit the use of space, while still incorporating plenty of entertainment for little miss fluffet.

SKIP TO MY LU(LU), MY DARLING

Name: Lulu bed (by Labbvenn)
Design: Renata Wites and Ada Brożyna (for Labbvenn)
Photography: Labbvenn

Every so often, there are moments when we find ourselves weighing a trade-off between style and comfort. Like women's shoes, for example. If it's "to die for," it'll be a killer for sure and you'll be screaming out a code blue on your pinky toe before the day is done. If it looks like Grammy's loafers, then you can be assured of a "walking on rose petals" experience.

Thankfully, pet furniture does not call for quite such drama. If it looks fashionable, it can be just as comfortable for your little furry rascal to sink his fluffy all into. The Lulu bed is a precise blend of refined style and unabashed comfort. Suited for a small pooch or a cat, the bed presents delightful snooze support packaged in subtle aesthetics that exude a slight retro-modern vibe (hence the name Lulu, perhaps?).

A quilted pillow nestles in an ash wood base with a wraparound backrest that makes the environment cozy and inviting for a languid cat or a sleepy li'l barker. It makes a great pet day bed in the living room or a corner pet lounge for a quick groom and breather before puss is off again on his all-important business of being fabulous. The Lulu bed is available in a variety of colors and can be matched with a Kikko table (page 122) in the same color to create a mini pet living room within your own living room.

UNDERCOVER COMFORT

Name: Kikko table (by Labbvenn)

Design: Renata Wites and Ada Brożyna (for Labbvenn)

Photography: Labbvenn

This table is a joy to both the cat and its designated attendant. Oops, the cat and *you*, we mean.

You will find pleasure in its simple elegance and your feline chief will pleasure in its comfortable cat hideout. The Kikko table reflects quintessential Scandinavian style in clean lines that flow seamlessly, without an over-cluttering of details. Its purist design is enhanced by its multifunctionality as a paws-and-people piece of furniture—our favorite kind—with a cat hammock tucked under the tabletop.

Made of a quilted fabric, the hammock makes a great place for kitty to go undercover (pun fully intended) and be undetected, being somewhat hidden, as she contemplates life, lunch, and your performance as cook, servant, and housekeeper.

As a table and a cat lounge in one, the Kikko table lets you and your independent feline relax together, even on the days when she's feeling a little less sociable and wants her own me(ow) time. The canopy-like feeling of the tabletop over the hammock creates a secure sanctuary where kitty can retreat to to unwind and unfurl her ruffled whiskers.

The hammock comes in four colors and can be easily unfastened and tossed into the machine to be laundered. The table in ash wood is easy to maintain and clean too. In a multi-cat or multi-species household, the Kikko table can be combined with the Lulu bed (page 118) in a matching color to extend sleeping options for your beloved furballs.

SNORING IN STYLE

Name: Loue bed (by Labbvenn)
Design: Mowo Studio (for Labbvenn)
Photography: Labbvenn

Watching our beloved pups sleep is one of our favorite things to do. When your pooch sleeps comfortably, you can manage just about everything else in your days comfortably. There is also much contentment to be had in watching your fuzzy-muzzle friend enjoying his sleep, the sound of his easy breaths rasping lightly through his wet puppy nose.

Good sleep begins with a healthy routine: nutritious food, ample exercise, and, of course, a good bed. The Loue dog bed not only emphasizes comfort with quality materials, but also highlights style with a sophisticated design that accentuates any modern interior.

This bed does not beat about the bush. Its design is straightforward in a simple, oval shape that provides ample room for your dog to lie down and get dreaming. The wooden base, made of beech from the Carpathian forests, extends up slightly on one side and finishes as a small headboard to support and cradle a leaning back for a cozy feeling; it also creates a snug crook to nuzzle into, should the fancy strike your canine buddy.

Filled with resilient foam, the mattress offers good support, even for larger dogs. The mattress fabric is as durable as it is breathable, to withstand that little extra "love" from pooch if he paws and scratches. Its excellent air permeability also keeps your canine cool as he snores the night away. The gray cover combined with the wood base completes a modern, yet warm, character that is fitting for an even warmer personality with whiskers, who will love the bed as much as he does you.

THE HIGH LIFE

Name: Three Poles Cat Tower
Design: Jiyoun Kim Studio
Photography: Nod lab

In some ancient cultures, cats were famously looked upon as gods. Therefore, it's perhaps not such a far-fetched notion to believe that the memory of this reverence somehow passed down in their DNA, contributing to your kitty's affinity for high perches where she can be transcendent and command that you worship her with that well-known, imperious cat glare.

The Three Poles Cat Tower is a platformed throne where kitty can bask in her eminence and impress upon you your good fortune to have her regal company. Keen design and functionality converse to compose a delicate form that respects your space while allowing your exalted feline to take to her high horse on scaffolds mounted all the way to the top.

Five round birch plywood rests notch three metal rods to form an engaging course for her royal highness to play, percolate plans, and pose. The platforms also provide comfortable lazing spots, offering options of cool wood or felted tops to occasionally simply pause and ponder. And when the day gets too dreary with admiration, a cushioned tray allows her to squeeze in a quick shut-eye between all the adulation.

Minimal in form, the cat tower contrasts its slim design with maximum considerations. A huge step away from the often bulky and boxy, carpet-covered designs of yesterday, the slim structure accommodates without difficulty to small spaces and tight corners, pleasing your demanding feline best when placed near a window, so she can look out at her kingdom below and take in the sights, while enjoying her high life.

COUCH PETATO

Name: Odense couch bed (by Weelywally)
Design: Onurhan Demir
Photography: Mustafa Ozbay

"My dog thinks he's human and my cat thinks he's a god." Of the many pet clichés that have come to be, this quote certainly rings true. If your tail-wagging friend has you asking, "Are you sure you are a dog?" then naturally, every creature comfort that you enjoy, pooch must have too: like a soft couch to flop onto, kick back, and just be … human.

The Odense couch bed is a picture of true comfort. Delightfully cozy and inviting by dog, cat, and people, standards, it will have you secretly wondering what it might feel like to throw your shoes off and sink into it yourself. It holds its own in your interior too, with stylish aplomb that is the work of a smart and trendy design.

An aluminum backrest cradles a plush back cushion that hugs a satisfyingly fluffy seat cushion. This joy is enhanced by side reclines formed by the wraparound backrest, making for a cozy lean-and-lie, or a scrumptiously sloppy slump-and-slide—whatever the style of your dog or cat. The cushioned wall also creates a sense of security and assurance for your scruffy snuffleupagus, so he can settle down contentedly feeling safe and protected.

Built to care for your fluffball, the bed avoids sharp edges and hard corners that can hurt a snoring sprawler; materials used are also free of chemicals to ensure a safe environment, so all your little buddy feels is love. With all this couch-ing and snuggling ahead, dare we say, even the cat might take time out from his lording to join in and be one of the guys—the canine-human variety, that is.

YOURS AND MINE

Name: Oslo (by Weelywally)
Design: Onurhan Demir
Photography: Mustafa Ozbay

It has been said that dog people and cat people are very different from each other. We don't know about that, but we are certainly glad that the folks who design pet furniture are only one type: animal lovers who care about furry beings and their comfort. Of course, weaving in style and elements of flair to indulge us pet guardians is great too, especially if it includes multifunctionality to create a paws-and-people piece.

The Oslo dog bed (cats can use it too) pleases pooch and you with its nifty fit as a side table in the living room, mug rest in your morning paper nook, or book stack beside your bed. The best part: it comes with an adorable puppy face that fronts a huge heart devoted unconditionally to you. Definitely hard to refuse.

Inspired by Japanese and Danish furniture designs, the Oslo forms clean, simple lines that pay attention to exacting soft corners and smooth edges to protect its furry inhabitant; this also serves to prevent any grazes that can occur as your cuddly canine sleeps with abandonment, blissfully unaware of lurking dangers.

This care also extends to the materials used, with natural wood and 100 percent cotton fabric ensuring that pooch's little corner is free of chemicals. The light aluminum body makes for easy cleaning and no-fuss transporting, because it's no secret that where you go, pooch goes too. To up the comfort factor further, the bed cushion is filled with premium quality fiber balls, so little waggy tail's dreams are as warm and fuzzy as he is.

IN DA HOUSE

Name: Small House Collection (by Weelywally)
Design: Onurhan Demir
Photography: Mustafa Ozbay

A multi-pet household is definitely an interesting one. Different personalities; sometimes different species; and a whole list of different ways to drive you up the wall. But we know you love it!

One of the many thrills of being surrounded by multiple pitter-pattering paws is styling napping arrangements for the lovelies when alone time is desired. Pet cribs that match along a base design, with their own style each, is a delightfully groovy concept, not to mention helpful to your interior decor, minimizing conspicuous eyesores.

Weelywally's Small House Collection offers three adorable designs for small dogs and cats. Playfully presented as houses, the Sydney, Volendam, and Wien pet beds will win the hearts of your furmily with their cozy interior and inviting sheltered designs that makes them feel snug and safe. Your heart is not spared either, for the sight of your furry angel soundly asleep in, literally, her very own tiny house is a ruthlessly endearing one, so get ready your "awwws."

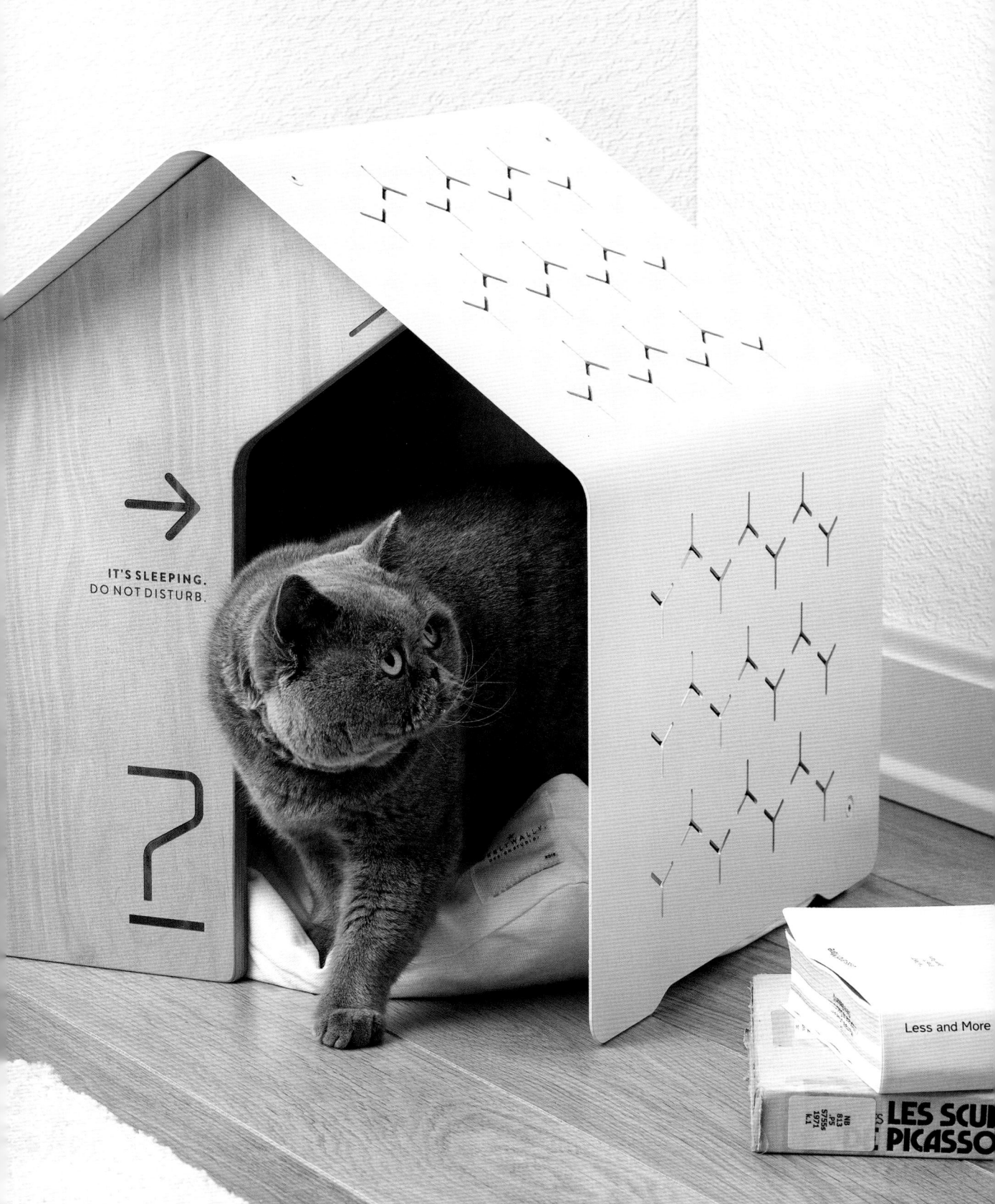

Available in an array of modern colors, the small houses feature straightforward, yet attractive, forms that are easy on the eyes. Taking inspiration from Dutch architecture and whimsical impressions, their stylish appearance blends amicably with all themes of decor, and won't clash with your home interior design scheme.

The Volendam and Wien designs even feature fabric sections that are interchangeable and available in a variety of colorful prints, so you can have some fun pairing different styles with different pet personalities. Of course, the cats, with their airs about them, will be less than impressed, but who's to say you can't indulge anyway.

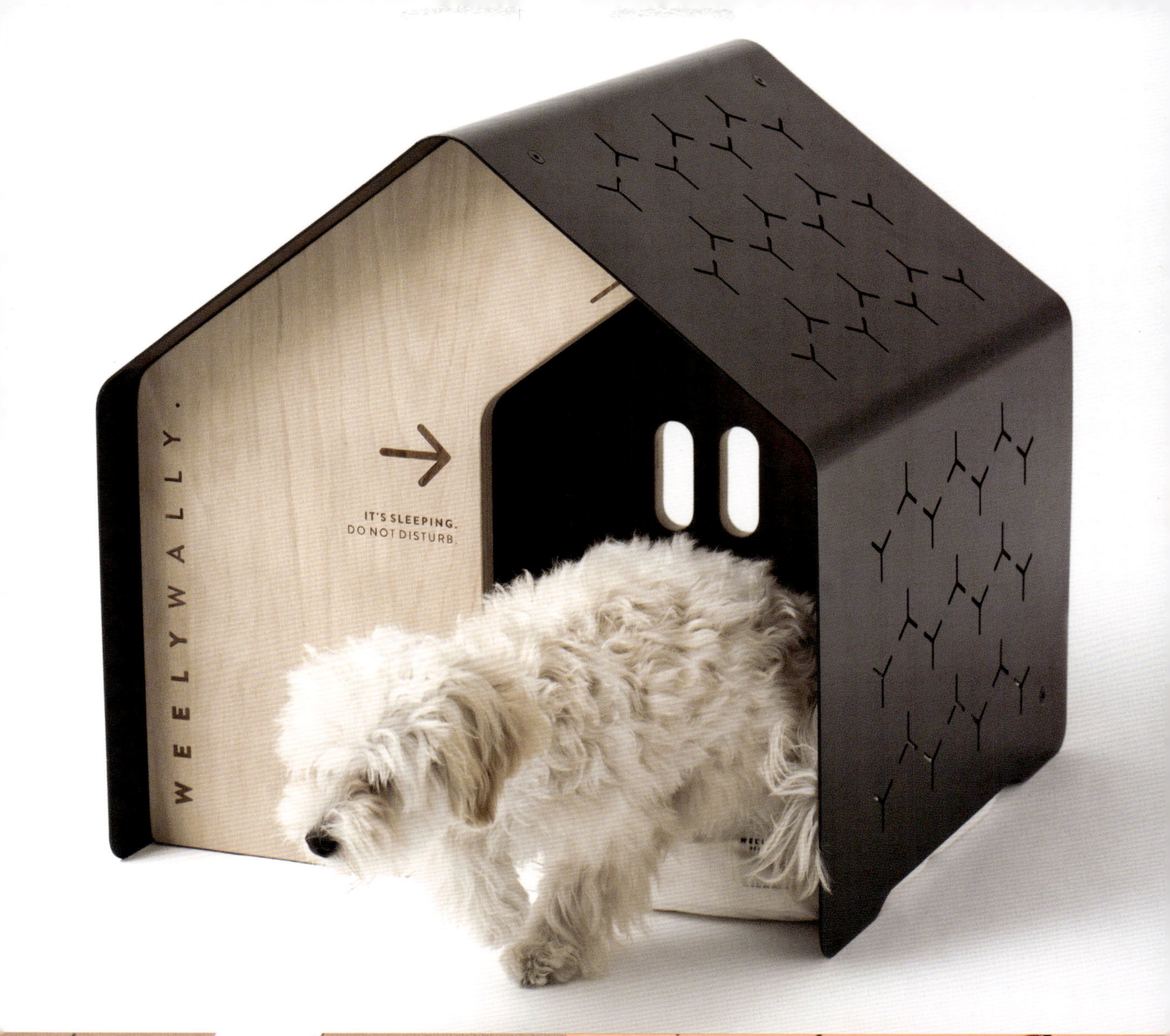
WEELYWALLY.
IT'S SLEEPING.
DO NOT DISTURB.

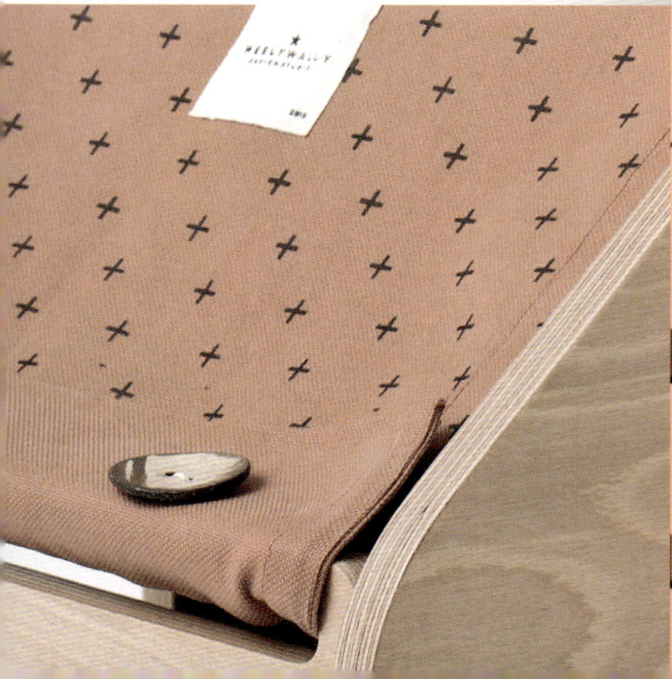

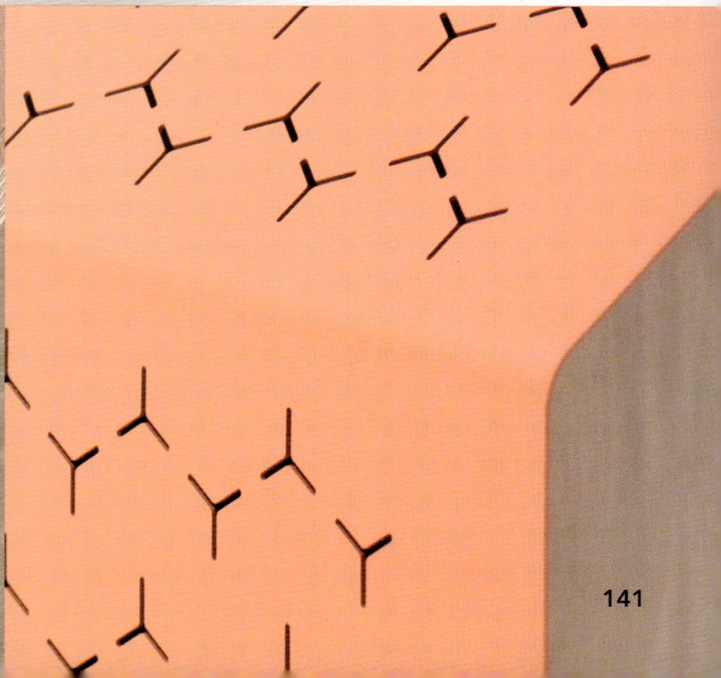

BEAM ME UP KITTY

Name: MYZOO Spaceship cat bed
Design: Everhu Industry Co. Ltd.
Photography: Everhu Industry Co. Ltd.

Have you noticed how cats like contorting themselves into curved spaces? They love arcs. And the Spaceship series of cat beds aims to please.

In warm, walnut veneer, the Spaceship series presents two different designs, Gamma and Alpha, that are modern, eco-friendly, and *space*-ious. The designs highlight a dome cover that lends an intergalactic space shuttle look to the beds, while providing a cozy, curved corner for cats to lean in, contort and curl up. Both designs are finished in wood with clear acrylic for the dome. The transparent dome on the beds allows any curious yet reserved moggy to be cocooned and feel safe, but still be able to see what is going on around her.

The Spaceship Alpha is a floor-standing, horizontally shaped bed, with domes on either end, and measures 25 inches (63 centimeters) in length and 16 inches (40 centimeters) in width. That's lots of curling up room; in fact, two cats can fit snugly in there without complaint.

The Spaceship Gamma is a more vertically shaped bed with a dome top and can either be placed on the floor or mounted on the wall to be combined with other MYZOO cat shelves (pages 174 and 184) to create a cat wall that provides your inquisitive felines with lots of entertainment, exercise, and nap nooks.

CATNAP CANOPY

Name: Canopy Bed
Design: Layer
Photography: Layer

This one is for the lovers of all things contemporary. A modern and stylish cat accessory, this bed is based not only on research into cat behavior, but also on user insights, so that pet people can reflect their own style in their snuggle puss's favorite things. And having pet accessories that will not cramp your personal style is definitely a plus in our book; not that anything about our lovable furballs could ever cramp our style.

Designed to connect with a new, modern generation of cat owners (oh, and the cat), the Canopy Bed prides itself on its expressive design, comfort, adaptability, and serving its master (the cat, not you). The bed can be adjusted according to three different configurations to provide a cozy sleeping area to fit the mood (again, the cat's, not yours). It can be a cave to scurry off into and hide in on a rainy day, or a cool lounge pad if kitty is feeling more sociable. The different styles not only provide kitty a variety of nap options, they also allow you to tune the visual detail to your mood.

The memory foam cushion is comfortable and a delight to snuggle into, and the canopy shell in PET material is durable enough to withstand scratching and any other unusual kitty expressions that cats are often known for. Available in three color options (Jungle, Tundra, and Savanna), the bed is a good example of being specially made for the unique needs of cats and thoughtfully designed for their people.

CAT-RIUM OF BEAMS

Name: Cat House
Design: SeijiIwamaArchitects
Photography: Seiji Iwama

The interior of this forty-year-old home in Japan was gutted and reconfigured to accommodate the lifestyle of its owners and their fun-loving cat. The living room is arranged on the second floor to enjoy a generous flooding of sunlight, where kitty can bask and delight in the many thrills of being a fine feline.

To heighten the thrill factor (literally), the usually dead space under the roof is revamped into a kitty highway. Instead of the flat ceiling often opted for in most Japanese houses, the ceiling is done away with entirely, exposing roof frames to create a kitty atrium with an adventure-loaded mass of beams where the cat can perch, stalk, or simply do her rounds to show off how awesome she is. Shelves are installed as stairs for kitty tc easily access its atrium playpen, and also because appearances must be maintained and a heritage of daintiness shall not be besmirched by ungainly clambering.

The stairs in the home were rebuilt to accommodate a litterbox room under the landing. A cat-sized square opening in the wall functions as a doorway for when kitty needs to visit the little kitty's room. A door lends privacy while the litterbox is in use and seals off any funky whiffs that might permeate. Another creative and cat-indulgent idea includes sisal rope wrapped around the base of a structural post to turn it into a nifty scratching pole. Many thoughtful designs come together in this house to make an inviting dwelling for kitty to call home.

FUREVER FUR-FREE

Name: Bye Bye Fur

Design: Hangzhou Furrytail Technology Co., Ltd.

Photography: Hangzhou Furrytail Technology Co., Ltd. and Shuzong (Haohaozhu)

A white cat on a gray bed? Bring it on!

Cats spend almost twenty hours a day sleeping and just like us, they appreciate a comfortable, cozy, and clean place to catch up on important snoozes. The Bye Bye Fur cat bed not only checks those three boxes, it is also stylish and elegant, designed around the universal language of classic geometry, ensuring no cat will turn its tiny triangle nose (or whiskers) up at it and walk away.

Fit for all seasons and interiors, the aesthetically pleasing, hemispherical design blends easily with all styles of decor, harmonizing nicely with any ensemble of furniture. It also superbly accommodates cats who love to curl up. The bed lining is made of merino wool from Australia, so your cat feels just like she's sleeping on clouds, snuggled in the soft down. For contrast, the stand on the white bed shell comes in options of gold, black, and white, adding some variation to the bed.

A specially tailored curved, silicone brush attachment keeps the bed fur-free as it rotates along the woolen surface to remove residual fluff. The brush takes away the problems sometimes associated with a material-based cat bed, making the job of cleaning it a breeze. As your little kitty saunters into her bed, rest assured in the knowledge that her hemisphere is always clean and fur-free.

SNAIL CAVE

Name: Little Snail
Design: Hangzhou Furrytail Technology Co., Ltd.
Photography: Hangzhou Furrytail Technology Co., Ltd.

Like people, every cat sleeps differently. Some like to sprawl on their backs—and on your side of the bed too with all four little limbs stretched out; some seek out a warm corner to curl in, tucked into themselves so expertly that you can't tell tail apart from tip of nose. Then there are some others that like to hide; you become convinced that they are lost until they magically appear and saunter into the kitchen come dinnertime.

The snail bed is perfect for those "vanishing" David Copperfield felines; they can "disappear," but still be present and under your nose, so you don't need to have a near coronary every time you can't find the cat. The shell of the snail makes a great cave for cats to hide in if they want to step out of the scene for a bit and relax without you. The plush, roomy interior that cocoons the cat in contentment also makes it feel secure and will appeal to every personality of cat, and possibly even you, though we don't advise you try to fit.

The soft base pad is thoughtfully created in dual-material finishes to accommodate different climate and temperatures. The long-fiber side keeps kitty warm and snug in colder months and the short-fiber side ensures no comfort is lost in warmer months, so kitty can still enjoy her cave hideout and make like she's not there. But this time, you can save yourself the search party and kick your legs up with a hot cuppa right beside her.

LEVEL-UP AND LET LOOSE

Name: Cat Time Cat Tree

Design: Hangzhou Furrytail Technology Co., Ltd.

Photography: Hangzhou Furrytail Technology Co., Ltd.

The best way to keep cats occupied and out of trouble is to give them their own space where they can let loose and be themselves without incurring the wrath of a tired-out, frazzled owner. With cats, it's all about territory and having their own will definitely ease anxiety and keep them from wreaking havoc in yours, especially when you lack the strength to even press "Start'"on the microwave to get that television dinner ready.

Making room for our pets in our lives, and our homes, is the most fundamental of expectations as pet guardians. The Cat Time Cat Tree is five levels of fun equipped with spacious spots to just chill and be a cat. Integrated into its interesting geometric design are corrugated surfaces to let the claws loose, platforms to ready themselves for pouncing, a hammock for snoozing without a care in the world, and dangle toys to paw around. There are also nooks and openings for your pampered feline to duck into and launch a game of hide-and-seek with you.

The open design lets you observe kitty's natural behavior and interact with her because an engaged, well-exercised kitty is a healthy kitty. Plus, who can resist a cat being all Bambi-eyed and cute as they pat at that fuzzy dangle toy, or roll over and gaze at you like you're the best person ever.

KITTY WALK-UP

Name: The Cat Flat

Design: Eleonor Moschevitz (for 24Storage)

Photography: Henrik Nero

Imagine how awesome it would be if your cat had its own flat complete with a television room, games room, lounge, and boudoir for grooming.

Great in compact living spaces, The Cat Flat takes into regard kitty's possible anxiety from being cooped up in a tiny area with little entertainment. And it looks pretty doing it.

Elegant in a wood finish, The Cat Flat is in essence a cabinet built as a kitty playground, with ramps, perches, portholes, and cubbyholes to keep your finicky feline engaged and away from destructive behavior. With input from Sweden's first cat psychologist, Susanne Hellman Holmström, this piece of furniture cares for the well-being of kitty without compromising on the aesthetics of your home interior.

The handcrafted cabinet displays a walnut veneer with lathed doors that lend grace to the obvious proportions of the piece. The doors can be left open or closed to create different types of ambiances for different play moods. When closed, the cat's movements can be glimpsed through the laths, creating a mysterious appeal that adds an interesting dimension to the decor.

The interior of The Cat Flat is composed in three levels, built almost like *Donkey Kong* game land. The first is a self-grooming station with a brush made from Forest Stewardship Council (FSC)-certified beech wood and boar bristles, and a scrub made from coconut fibers. The other levels make up play and rest areas that feature sisal mats, eco-certified lambskin, and leather. There is even a tablet mount so your discerning feline can watch *Finding Nemo* as she settles down for a well-deserved snooze after lunch.

OH, BUSY ME(OW)

Name: MYZOO Busycat ottoman and shelf

Design: Everhu Industry Co. Ltd.

Photography: Everhu Industry Co. Ltd.

Now, which cat person does not like being around their furry friends all the time? That's right, none of us.

Stylish yet practical furniture made to serve both our pets as well as ourselves is always ideal in such households where pet and person love spending time with each other. The MYZOO Busycat range showcases a functional ottoman and cat shelves to create a space that is ideal for both species and the range of preferences and personalities they come with.

The ottoman has a cushioned seat top and a hollowed center that makes an ideal cat snuggle spot. The cool bit: the cushion top doubles as a cat scratching board, or can be removed to transform the ottoman's seat-top to a tabletop, to create a convenient coffee table, or side table. The hexagonal shape of the ottoman affords a modular character to the piece so that you can join multiple pieces to create your own unique furniture design.

In a matching hexagonal design, the MYZOO Busycat shelves create a fun cat wall for the cat to play about. With four openings on the sides, the units can be joined together to create an interesting catwalk or hive-like structure for the cats to climb and get some exercise in (which we know many of our pampered princes and princesses could do with), while also having fun.

Made of pine, these cat shelves add warmth to almost any decor and work well in small spaces and apartments for our lovely kitties to get busy and launch into playtime.

OUT ON THE TABLE

Name: CATable 2.0
Design: LYCS Architecture
Photography: LYCS Architecture

Multifunctional pet furniture that also serves people is a joy. It is even better if it's customizable. Enter CATable 2.0.

The new, very much updated (and, dare we say, upgraded) version of the CATable 1.0 bears a resemblance to the earlier version only in its offering of fun for your curious kitty. An almost deconstructed version of the first CATable, version 2.0 steps away from an actual table design, breaking the form to present itself as a system of four wood blocks with different designs. And therein lies its cool factor, because now it can be customized to be a furniture piece of your design, desire, and need.

Arrange a bookshelf, put together a bench, or even fashion a plant stand. As much entertainment and fun as you have designing creative pieces that lift your decor, kitty will have playing on the CATable 2.0. Like the earlier table version, tunnels and openings adorn every piece, so your curious furry munchkin will have a ball crawling through the spaces, peeking about, and exploring the passageways. To really make an impression in your decor and win "best person of the year," join a collection of CATable 2.0 systems to create fascinating play tunnels that divert up, down, left, right, and everywhere, which kitty will love, and love you even more for.

SHELVE IT

Name: Luna, Twinkle Star, and Moku
Design: Everhu Industry Co. Ltd.
Photography: Everhu Industry Co. Ltd.

Play is a big part of every cat's day. A cat who has gotten enough playtime and entertainment rests easy and rests well.

The Luna, Twinkle Star, and Moku wall-mounted cat shelves help expand the world of our little furry pals with a host of interesting elements to occupy their days with. Easily mounted at any height, they indulge cats' natural behavior to be perched high, hawk-eyeing the day's activities below them.

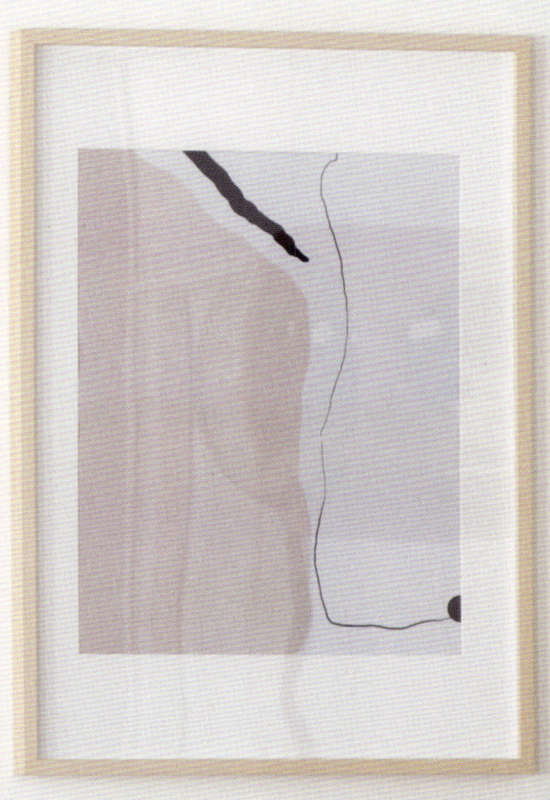

The crescent-shaped Luna shelf creates a comfortable rest platform with its inclined base, which cats love as it fits with their much-loved propped-up-against resting posture. You know the one we're talking about—where their elbows are always propped on a cushion; a book; a pile of folded laundry even, as they peer into your soul. Yep, that's the one. Place this shelf beside a window and it's happy days for your little royalty as she gets comfortable, propped on her dandy perch, watching the world go by.

Expand the catification with the Twinkle Star scratch pole and Moku cloud shelf, which come in the shape of a star and err … cloud, respectively.

The complementing designs create a theme and jazz up your home interior with a touch of playfulness. The Moku shelf also has a transparent, acrylic base, which will be sure to provide loads of entertainment for a multi-cat furmily as they get up to their usual antics climbing, exploring, and peering curiously at each other through the see-through base. All the curiosity with zero the danger. That's definitely a win.

IT'S FETCHING BRILLIANT

Name: Fetch House (Architecture for Dogs)

Design: CallisonRTKL

Photography: CallisonRTKL / Dustin Wekesser

"I made it myself," are the first words you'll use to describe this eye-catching and interesting doghouse when someone asks, because what could be more fulfilling than building your pooch a home with your own hands—well, a 3D printer and your hands, but it still counts.

Modeled through digital design and 3D-printing fabrication, the Fetch House is built on a modular structure that is customizable; it can easily be tailored to the size of your dog based on simple measurement inputs in the digital script. It can also "grow" with your pup by easily adding modules to expand it. Once the structure is complete, then comes the fun part, designing a pattern of your choice with repurposed tennis balls.

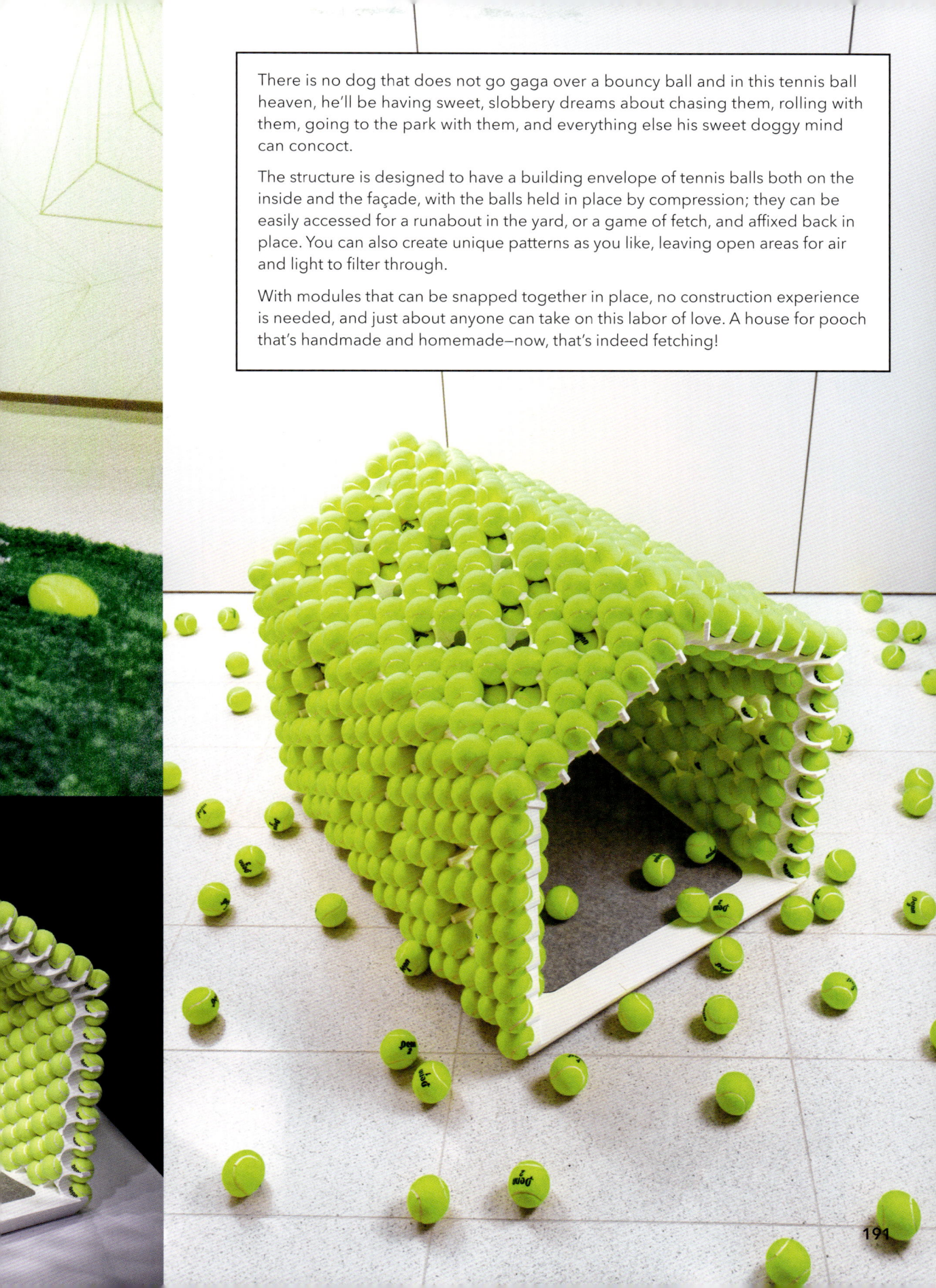

There is no dog that does not go gaga over a bouncy ball and in this tennis ball heaven, he'll be having sweet, slobbery dreams about chasing them, rolling with them, going to the park with them, and everything else his sweet doggy mind can concoct.

The structure is designed to have a building envelope of tennis balls both on the inside and the façade, with the balls held in place by compression; they can be easily accessed for a runabout in the yard, or a game of fetch, and affixed back in place. You can also create unique patterns as you like, leaving open areas for air and light to filter through.

With modules that can be snapped together in place, no construction experience is needed, and just about anyone can take on this labor of love. A house for pooch that's handmade and homemade—now, that's indeed fetching!

OFF WITH HIS CAGE

Name: PAWD (Happy pet nesting space)
Design: KindTail
Photography: KindTail

Your pet's home within your home is more important than you know. While your lovable fluffball might love being around you, a place to call his own creates security and builds confidence, especially when you're not at home. In training, it also fosters discipline and conditions good behavior. It's a different ball game with cats though: they train us, but that conversation is a whole other book altogether, so for now, back to the soft muzzles we adore.

Dog crates are often not the prettiest of houses, being cold, grim metal cages. So Amy Kim, founder of KindTail, fixed that.

Born out of needing a comfortable doggy home for her very own pooch, PAWD is the very opposite of a metal cage. In fact, its design takes inspiration from its very function—a crate. Genius. Built from ABS plastic, it's lighter, easier to move around, and not a chore to dismantle.

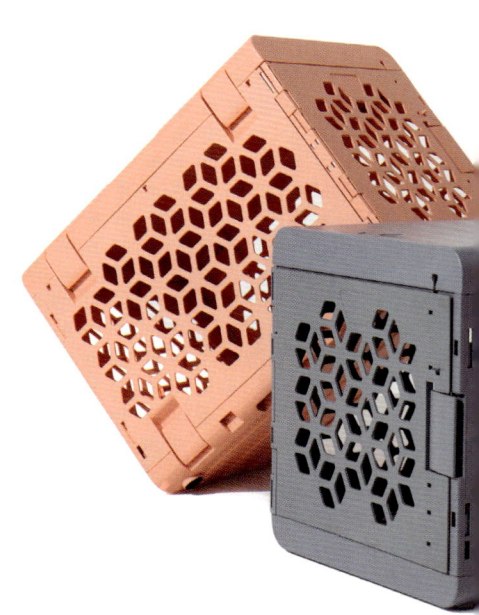

Oh, but PAWD is unique too. It's the first of its kind to have a detachable top and sides that fold into the base of the nesting space. In short, when dismantled it folds into a neat plastic box—reminiscent of a drill case—not bigger than the size of a newspaper folded in half. How's that for cool? It's certainly worlds away from the hideous metal monstrosity you have to camouflage behind the drapes.

Pooch will love it too, with its cozy confines that do not feel like a cell. Available in two sizes and three colors (gray, pink, or white), it almost disappears in your interior, easily passing off for a side table—until you notice the side table has a tail.

PEEKABOO, I SEE YOU

Name: Holey Moley
Design: Asolidplan
Photography: 0StudioSg

How does a family with two young children and two cats keep their lovable motley crew entertained? Play peekaboo, of course.

Requests for a cozy home with generous open space to accommodate the play of both little feet and little paws sets little windows of surprises that delight by creating opportunities for playful interactions, while enhancing the decor.

The home design cleverly transforms the often static, transitional corridor space with recessed and extending square shelves in various sizes that make for a great kitty playground as they duck, dive, and dally. These squares become hiding spots to lie-in-wait in and plan surprise attacks, while the shelf tops become mini mountain plateaus to poise on for a pounce on unsuspecting feet, or a furry cat head! We are obliged to add that the shelves are also meant to display decorative ornaments and are not just for the cats, as they would like to have you think.

Customized sliding panels turn the shelves into open windows, enhancing and widening the play area for an all-out round of cat-and-seek as the sly twitchy tails duck into new-found hiding spots. The open windows also allow interaction between the cats and their humans, and their little humans, maybe even enticing a cheeky game of peekaboo—now you see those pointy ears, and now you don't!

When all are played out, the shelves turn into elevated nap platforms, just right for a shut-eye with a view, not to mention, also well-placed to lure a passing human for a loving nuzzle or a scratch behind the ears. Well played, indeed.

REFLECTIONS OF LOVE

Name: Yololand
Design: Rooot Studio Pte Ltd
Photography: Charmaine Oh

When your loyal canine is family, you share everything, wanting your scruffy pawrtner in crime to have everything that you do. A home designed just for your loving pooch with the same stylish implements as yours is right up the alley of dog lovers, and it says clearly, "you and I are one and the same."

This Singapore family shows their doggy member that paws and people are one, with a specially designed doghouse built as part of the home design. Among bold and playful interior statements, a cozy alcove for pooch is integrated into the main living space, so that the happy tail-thumper is always a part of the activities and together with the pack.

This personal paw space is cleverly created under a recessed seat that performs in part as a shoe stool, and which extends from the shoe cabinet. The multifunctional character of the installation saves space, while creatively optimizing it within the seamless decor.

As important as pooch is, so is his house, as it mimics the anchor accent that defines the home's interior division. The pitched entryway that introduces the private bedroom area also introduces pooch's sanctu*pawry*, with an entrance that finishes in a pitched top. Symbolizing a tent, this design reflects the family's love for adventure and the outdoors, and adds a personalized nuance to both the home and the doghouse. The echoing of this dedicated pattern not only ensures a flow of key design notes, it also allocates prominence to the doghouse and the presence of the household's darling furball. But above all, it says, "this pooch is with me; he's family!"

IN THE CENTER OF IT ALL

Name: Sheridan Residence
Design: StudioAC
Photography: Sarjoun Faour

Needless to say, for us pet people, home is where the paw is. And this home in Toronto, Canada shouts it out loud and proud, with a doghouse built into its very core as a focal point in the design.

This paws-and-people home conceives an interior that revolves around a plywood insertion, which accommodates storage needs for the family, hides the staircase, and most importantly, shows Rusty how much he is loved, with a doghouse built right into it.

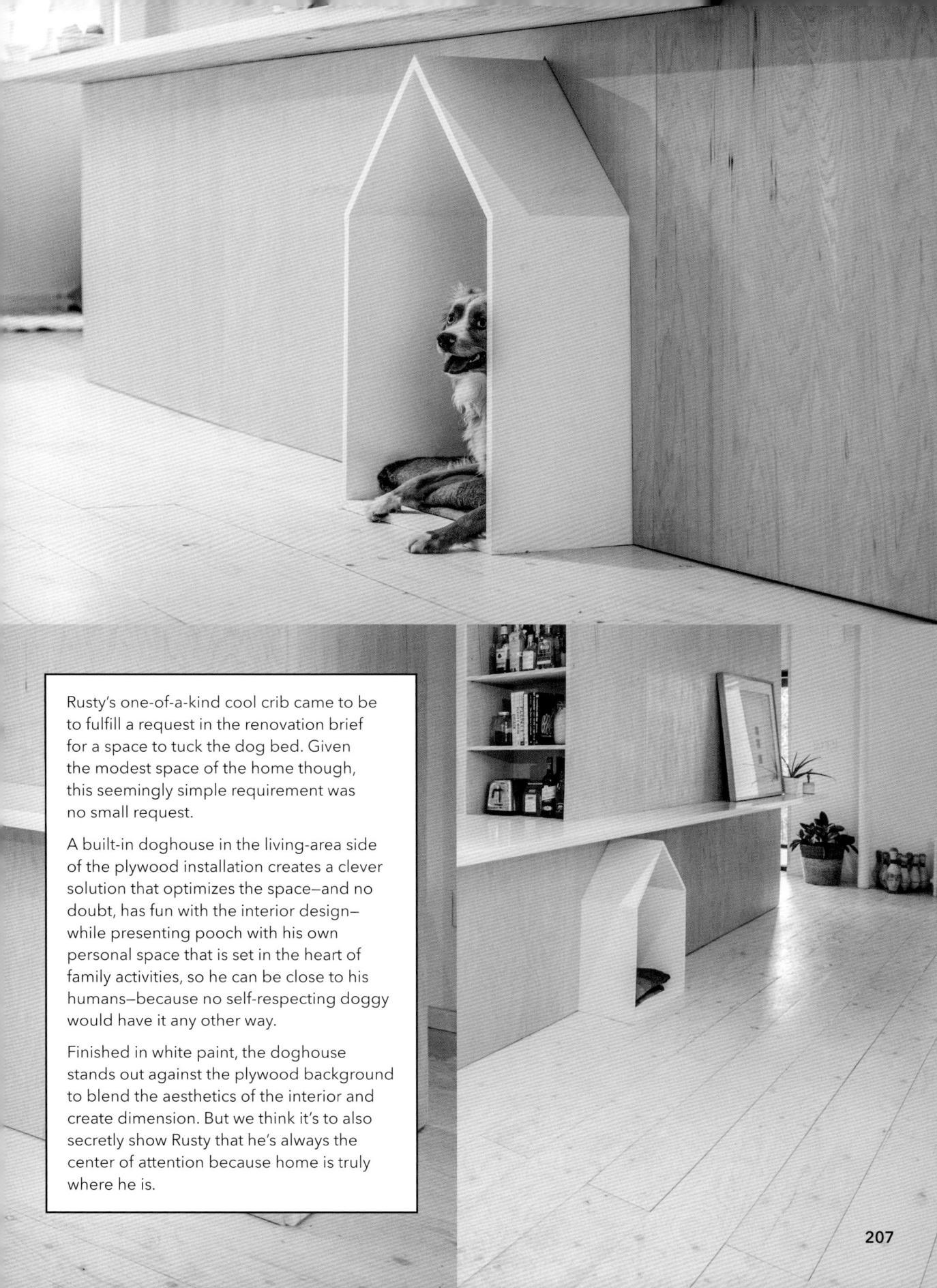

Rusty's one-of-a-kind cool crib came to be to fulfill a request in the renovation brief for a space to tuck the dog bed. Given the modest space of the home though, this seemingly simple requirement was no small request.

A built-in doghouse in the living-area side of the plywood installation creates a clever solution that optimizes the space—and no doubt, has fun with the interior design—while presenting pooch with his own personal space that is set in the heart of family activities, so he can be close to his humans—because no self-respecting doggy would have it any other way.

Finished in white paint, the doghouse stands out against the plywood background to blend the aesthetics of the interior and create dimension. But we think it's to also secretly show Rusty that he's always the center of attention because home is truly where he is.

UNDER THE BRIDGE

Name: sHome
Design: Linear Space Concepts
Photography: See Chee Keong

How do you keep three cats entertained in an apartment? Build a high cat bridge. And how do you keep yourself entertained alongside the cats? Give the bridge a glass bottom, so you can look up at the cute underside of dainty kitty paws making their crossing.

Custom-carpentry, designer furniture, and a creative collision of colors, textures, and patterns all come together in this Singapore apartment to build a vibrant, boutique hotel-style home for a couple and their kitty clan. Hues of turquoise and green rule the home appearance and flow into prominent design details, like the statement cat bridge.

Defining this home, the bridge announces loud and proud, "Cats live here!" and provides the many paws in the household space and freedom to play and enjoy high viewpoints that felines so love. The transparent base, playful as it is, also serves a higher purpose: it enables visual contact between the felines and their humans, while also presenting opportunities for cheeky "you can see, but you can't touch" play, strengthening bonds between pet and person through these interactions.

Of course, there is also the amusement factor of observing one's cats from a quirky angle, such as from below them, speaking to the fun-loving character of the resident humans.

As gaze-grabbing as the cat bridge is, it also highlights a clever use of space and design smarts, staggering into special kitty steps that join with the television console to create additional storage and cleverly tuck away wire clutter, so nothing gets in the way as cat be nimble, cat be swift, running about and enjoying their one-of-a-kind cat-perfect home.

HAVEN OF HARMONY

Name: Cats at Prince Charles
Design: Linear Space Concepts
Photography: See Chee Keong

As a cat guardian, it's not surprising to sometimes chance upon your finicky critter catching a snooze in unusual spots—like under the television sideboard; in the laundry hamper; or even in the bathroom—even though they have their dedicated beds. This family indulges this peculiar whim, but without cramping the humans' style. Through trendy decor polishes and inventive design, this time, the "unusual" becomes intentional.

The watchword in this Singapore home is "coexistence." Humans and kitties live together happily and comfortably—translation: lots of engagement for the cats, but no obstacle courses of cumbersome cat furniture that the humans need to maneuver around.

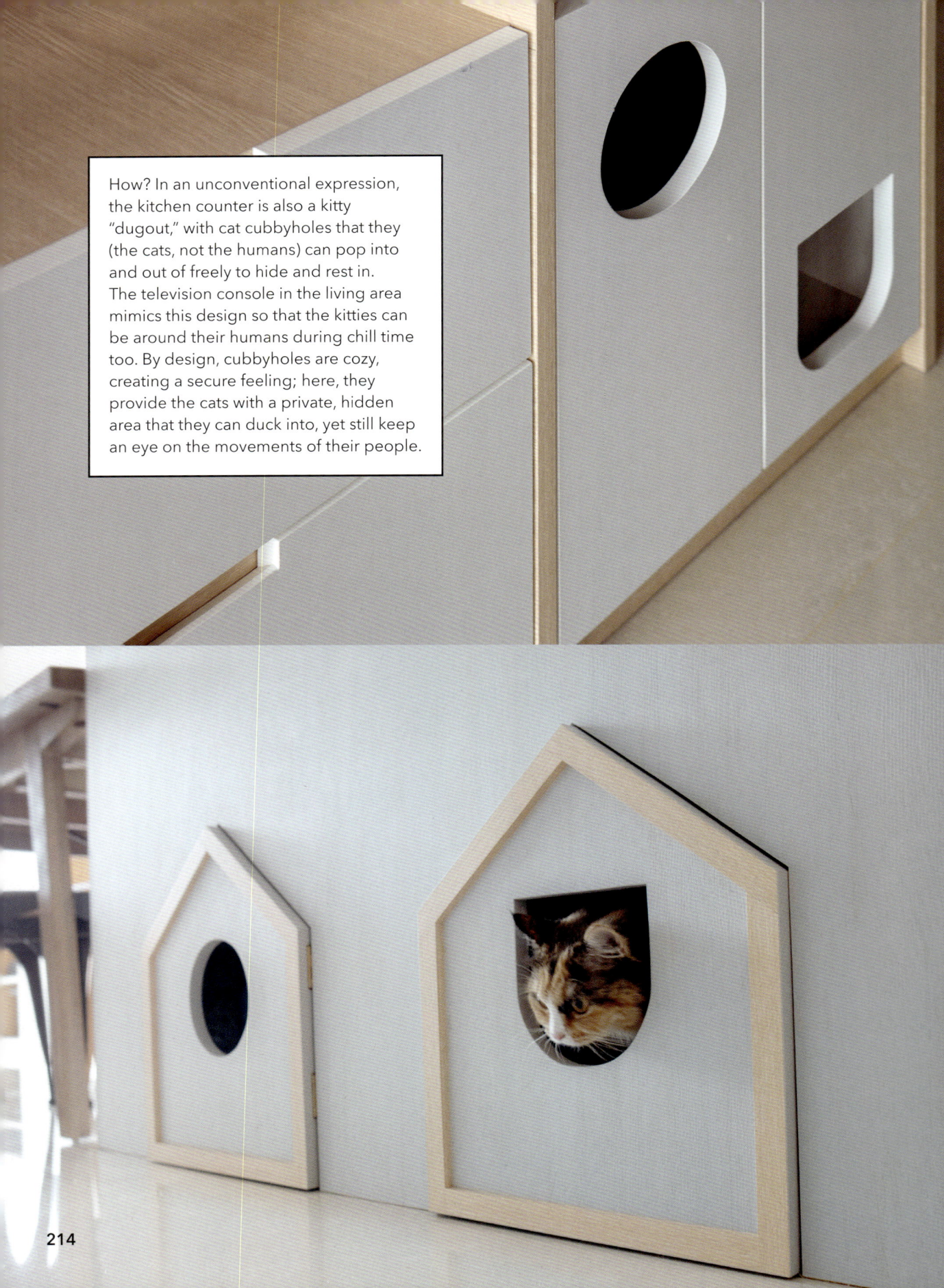

How? In an unconventional expression, the kitchen counter is also a kitty "dugout," with cat cubbyholes that they (the cats, not the humans) can pop into and out of freely to hide and rest in. The television console in the living area mimics this design so that the kitties can be around their humans during chill time too. By design, cubbyholes are cozy, creating a secure feeling; here, they provide the cats with a private, hidden area that they can duck into, yet still keep an eye on the movements of their people.

Open shelves next to the dining area cater to more sociable, playful moods. Arranged at different heights, they indulge the kitties' natural tendencies to climb and explore. The humans have use of them too, of course, for display and storage, for what could be more warming than coming home to the sight of a cat napping cozily on a shelf, a paw dangling lazily, next to some books and a lush houseplant.

ELECTRIC WITHOUT WIRES

Name: Norrom Aquarium
Design: Törnros & Co
Photography: Törnros & Co

The home you create for your fish becomes their world, and like any self-respecting pet guardian, you spare no effort to make that world beautiful and suited to their needs. And so you eventually sit, enjoying your hours-long fish-gazing against a wire-web backdrop that trails to an extension socket, which snakes to a power point somewhere to power the appliances of this aqueous home.

Aquariums with wire tentacles have become accepted as part and parcel—a tolerated blemish in your home decor to enjoy the tranquil beauty of fish therapy. The Norrom Aquarium challenges that norm in a purist Scandinavian design that adds to, rather than subtracts from, your home interior; it will have even your fishes doing the *fin*dango.

The first defiance begins in form. Countering conventional angular shapes is an upright cylindrical body capped with trims—a lid and a base. Hand-crafted in a selection of classic and exotic woods, these limited-edition trims are interchangeable to match the color scheme of your fishy community. Oh, and your decor, of course. There is even a template to 3D-print your own design.

The real show-stopper is the hidden, or integrated, lighting and filtration system that eliminates pesky dangling wires. Set in the base of the tank, these systems are designed to perform, leave you with nothing more to want.

The bubble tube displays a snazzy bubble show that lifts the entire performance, together with adjustable lighting (500 lumens at maximum) that can be dimmed or increased to preference. The only thing the Norrom Aquarium leaves is to enjoy its clean, simple, and concise beauty, made spectacular with your colorful fishy friends.

*All new aquariums must be cycled for the comfort of your new fishy family and should not be over capacity—one gallon of water per fin is an acceptable allocation. Fresh plants help the bio climate of your aquarium and create hiding spots, which the fishes will most certainly appreciate.

Project Credits

CIRCLE OF LOVE 10-15
360 Villa · 123DV
123dv.nl
Photography Hannah Anthonysz

ON THE CATWALK 16-21
Anti-earthquake Cat House · Hitotomori Architects
hitotomori.net
Photography Hiroki Kawata

MI CASA, SU CASA 22-25
NeconoMa · Alegre Design (for Katzden Architec)
alegredesign.es
Photography Pablo Bosch

A WALK OF FUN 26-31
Casa de Gatos · WOWOWA Architecture
wowowa.com.au
Photography Martina Gemmola

BOX-IN AND CHILL OUT 32-35
pidan cat bed · pidan
pidan.com/en
Photography pidan

GET CLIMBING 36-39
Geometric Climber-6 Gratings (cat tree) · pidan
pidan.com/en
Photography pidan

CHERRY ON THE CAKE 40-43
Cupcake pet bed · pidan
pidan.com/en
Photography pidan

SWINGING GOOD TIME 44-47
Hammock pet bed · pidan
pidan.com/en
Photography pidan

EARTH TO POOCH, OVER 48-51
Heads or Tails · nendo
nendo.jp
Photography Akihiro Yoshida

WHAT A SQUARE 52-55
Cubic pet goods · nendo
nendo.jp
Photography Akihiro Yoshida

FIT FOR ROYALTY 56-59
Cat's Moving Castle · Hangzhou Furrytail Technology Co., Ltd.
furrytail-pet.com
Photography Hangzhou Furrytail Technology Co., Ltd.

HOME-IN-ONE 60-63
D&C House · Kononenko ID
kononenkoid.com
Photography Andrii Podorozhny

NOOK FOR POOCH 64-69
Withrow Laneway House · Studio North
studionorth.ca
Photography Studio North

PUSS IN BOOKS 70-75
House for Booklovers and Cats · Barker Associates Architecture Office
baaostudio.com
Photography Francis Dzikowski

A CUT ABOVE 76-79
Niku Rug (Architecture for Dogs) · MAD Architects
i-mad.com
Photography Hiroshi Yoda

ALL ACCESS PASS 80-83
Sacha Apartment · SABO project
sabo-project.com
Photography Alexandre Delaunay

AWAKEN THE WILD 84-87
Juggernaut · Catastrophic Creations
catastrophiccreations.com
Photography Michael Wilson

CHAMBER OF SECRET FUN 88-91
Neko Modern Cat Tree · Yoh Komiyama Design
yohkomiyama.com
Photography Tomooki Kengaku

CORRUGATED PARADISE 92-97
Room Collection · A Cat Thing
acatthing.com
Photography Heycheese

FULL HOUSE 98-103
Pets Playground · Sim-Plex Design Studio
sim-plex-design.com
Photography Patrick Lam

HAVING A BALL 104-9
The Cube, The Ball · Meyou Paris
meyouparis.com
Photography Meyou Paris

HOW ABOUT A LIFT? 110-13
The Bed · Meyou Paris
meyouparis.com
Photography Meyou Paris

KITTY FROM THE BLOCK 114-17
Kitty Kasas Collection (by Kitty Kasas) · Studio Mango
studiomango.nl
Photography Kitty Kasas

SKIP TO MY LU(LU), MY DARLING 118-21
Lulu bed (by Labbvenn) · Renata Wites and Ada Brożyna (for Labbvenn)
labbvenn.com
Photography Labbvenn

UNDERCOVER COMFORT 122–25
Kikko table (by Labbvenn) · Renata Wites and Ada Brożyna (for Labbvenn)
labbvenn.com
Photography Labbvenn

SNORING IN STYLE 126–29
Loue bed (by Labbvenn) · Mowo Studio (for Labbvenn)
mowostudio.pl
Photography Labbvenn

THE HIGH LIFE 130–33
Three Poles Cat Tower · Jiyoun Kim Studio
jiyounkim.com
Photography Nod lab

COUCH PETATO 134–35
Odense couch bed (by Weelywally) · Onurhan Demir
weelywally.com
Photography Mustafa Ozbay

YOURS AND MINE 136–37
Oslo (by Weelywally) · Onurhan Demir
weelywally.com
Photography Mustafa Ozbay

IN DA HOUSE 138–41
Small House Collection (by Weelywally) · Onurhan Demir
weelywally.com
Photography Mustafa Ozbay

BEAM ME UP KITTY 142–47
MYZOO Spaceship cat bed · Everhu Industry Co. Ltd.
myzoostudio.com
Photography Everhu Industry Co. Ltd.

CATNAP CANOPY 148–51
Canopy Bed · Layer
layerdesign.com
Photography Layer

CAT-RIUM OF BEAMS 152–55
Cat House · SeijiIwamaArchitects
sia08.com
Photography Seiji Iwama

FUREVER FUR-FREE 156–59
Bye Bye Fur · Hangzhou Furrytail Technology Co., Ltd.
furrytail-pet.com
Photography Hangzhou Furrytail Technology Co., Ltd. and Shuzong (Haohaozhu)

SNAIL CAVE 160–63
Little Snail · Hangzhou Furrytail Technology Co., Ltd.
furrytail-pet.com
Photography Hangzhou Furrytail Technology Co., Ltd.

LEVEL-UP AND LET LOOSE 164–67
Cat Time Cat Tree · Hangzhou Furrytail Technology Co., Ltd.
furrytail-pet.com
Photography Hangzhou Furrytail Technology Co., Ltd.

KITTY WALK-UP 168–73
The Cat Flat · Eleonor Moschevitz (for 24Storage)
designfolder.se
Photography Henrik Nero

OH, BUSY ME(OW) 174–79
MYZOO Busycat ottoman and shelf · Everhu Industry Co. Ltd.
myzoostudio.com
Photography Everhu Industry Co. Ltd.

OUT ON THE TABLE 180–83
CATable 2.0 · LYCS Architecture
lycs-arc.com
Photography LYCS Architecture

SHELVE IT 184–87
Luna, Twinkle Star, and Moku · Everhu Industry Co. Ltd.
myzoostudio.com
Photography Everhu Industry Co. Ltd.

IT'S FETCHING BRILLIANT 188–91
Fetch House (Architecture for Dogs) · CallisonRTKL
callisonrtkl.com
Photography CallisonRTKL / Dustin Wekesser

OFF WITH HIS CAGE 192–95
PAWD (Happy pet nesting space) · KindTail
kindtail.com
Photography KindTail

PEEKABOO, I SEE YOU 196–99
Holey Moley · Asolidplan
asolidplan.sg
Photography 0StudioSg

REFLECTIONS OF LOVE 200–3
Yololand · Rooot Studio Pte Ltd
roootstudio.com
Photography Charmaine Oh

IN THE CENTER OF IT ALL 204–7
Sheridan Residence · StudioAC
archcollab.com
Photography Sarjoun Faour

UNDER THE BRIDGE 208–11
sHome · Linear Space Concepts
linearspaceconcepts.com
Photography See Chee Keong

HAVEN OF HARMONY 212–17
Cats at Prince Charles · Linear Space Concepts
linearspaceconcepts.com
Photography See Chee Keong

ELECTRIC WITHOUT WIRES 218–21
Norrom Aquarium · Törnros & Co
tornros.co
Photography Törnros & Co